THE COLD WAR

A Political and Diplomatic History of the Modern World

THE COLD WAR

Edited by Meredith Day

Britannica
Educational Publishing
IN ASSOCIATION WITH

ROSEN
EDUCATIONAL SERVICES

Published in 2017 by Britannica Educational Publishing (a trademark of Encyclopædia Britannica, Inc.) in association with The Rosen Publishing Group, Inc. 29 East 21st Street, New York, NY 10010

Distributed exclusively by Rosen Publishing.
To see additional Britannica Educational Publishing titles, go to rosenpublishing.com.

First Edition

Britannica Educational Publishing
J.E. Luebering: Director, Core Reference Group
Anthony L. Green: Editor, Compton's by Britannica

Rosen Publishing
Meredith Day: Editor
Nelson Sá: Art Director
Matt Cauli: Designer
Cindy Reiman: Photography Manager
Bruce Donnola: Photo Research

Library of Congress Cataloging-in-Publication Data

Names: Day, Meredith. | Britannica Educational Publishing.
Title: The Cold War / edited by Meredith Day.
Description: First edition. | New York : Britannica Educational Publishing in
  association with Rosen Educational Services, 2017. | Series: A political
  and diplomatic history of the modern world | Audience: Grades 7 to 12. |
  Includes bibliographical references and index.
Identifiers: LCCN 2015048889 | ISBN 9781680483581 (library bound : alkaline
  paper)
Subjects: LCSH: Cold War—Juvenile literature. | World
  politics—1945–1989—Juvenile literature.
Classification: LCC D843 .C577243 2017 | DDC 909.82—dc23
LC record available at http://lccn.loc.gov/2015048889

Manufactured in China

Contents

Introduction

Following the surrender of Nazi Germany in May 1945 near the close of World War II, the uneasy wartime alliance between the United States and Great Britain on the one hand and the Soviet Union on the other began to unravel. By 1948 the Soviets had installed left-wing governments in the countries of eastern Europe that had been liberated by the Red Army. The Americans and the British feared the permanent Soviet domination of eastern Europe and the threat of Soviet-influenced communist parties coming to power in the democracies of western Europe. The Soviets, on the other hand, were determined to maintain control of eastern Europe in order to safeguard against any possible renewed threat from Germany, and they were intent on spreading communism worldwide, largely for ideological reasons.

Thus began the Cold War, the open yet restricted rivalry that developed after World War II between the United States and the Soviet Union and their respective allies. The Cold War was waged on political, economic, and propaganda fronts and had only limited recourse to weapons. The term was first used by the English writer George Orwell in an article published in 1945 to refer to what he predicted would be a nuclear stalemate between "two or three monstrous super-states, each possessed of a weapon by which millions of people can be wiped out in a few seconds." It was first used in the United States by the American financier and presidential adviser Bernard Baruch in a speech at the State House in Columbia, South Carolina, in 1947. The Cold War had solidified by 1947–48, when U.S. aid provided under the Marshall Plan to western Europe had brought those countries under American influence and the Soviets had installed openly communist regimes in eastern Europe.

The Soviet Union essentially sealed off itself and its dependent eastern and central European allies from open contact with the West and other noncommunist areas, a political, military, and ideological barrier often referred to as the Iron Curtain. The term Iron Curtain had been in occasional and varied use as a metaphor since the 19th century, but it came to prominence only after it was used by the former British prime minister Winston Churchill in a speech at Fulton, Missouri, on March 5, 1946, when he said of the communist states, "From Stettin in the Baltic to Trieste in the Adriatic, an iron curtain has descended across the Continent."

The Cold War reached its peak in 1948–53. In this period the Soviets unsuccessfully blockaded the Western-held sectors of West Berlin (1948–49); the United States and its European allies formed the North Atlantic Treaty Organization (NATO), a unified military command to resist the Soviet presence in Europe (1949); the Soviets exploded their first atomic warhead (1949), thus ending the American monopoly on the atomic bomb; the Chinese communists came to power in mainland China (1949); and the Soviet-supported communist government of North Korea invaded U.S.-supported South Korea in 1950, setting off an indecisive Korean War that lasted until 1953.

From 1953 to 1957 Cold War tensions relaxed somewhat, largely owing to the death of the longtime Soviet dictator Joseph Stalin in 1953; nevertheless, the standoff remained. A unified military organization among the Soviet-bloc countries, the Warsaw Pact, was formed in 1955; West Germany was admitted into NATO that same year.

Another intense stage of the Cold War was in 1958–62. In 1961, in order to stop the exodus of 2.5 million East Germans

Soldiers lay bricks to build up the Berlin Wall in 1961.

who had fled to West Germany via West Berlin, East Germany built a barrier to close off East Germans' access to West Berlin. The Berlin Wall represented a physical manifestation of the metaphorical Iron Curtain and thus became a symbol of the Cold War as a whole.

Meanwhile, the United States and the Soviet Union began developing intercontinental ballistic missiles, and in 1962 the Soviets began secretly installing missiles in Cuba that could be used to launch nuclear attacks on U.S. cities. This sparked the Cuban missile crisis (1962), a confrontation that brought the two superpowers to the brink of war before an agreement was reached to withdraw the missiles. The Cuban missile crisis showed that neither the United States nor the Soviet Union were ready to use nuclear weapons for fear of the other's retaliation (and thus of mutual atomic annihilation). The two superpowers soon signed the Nuclear Test-Ban Treaty of 1963, which banned aboveground nuclear weapons testing. But the crisis also hardened the Soviets' determination never again to be humiliated by their military inferiority, and they began a buildup of both conventional and strategic forces that the United States was forced to match for the next 25 years.

Throughout the Cold War the United States and the Soviet Union avoided direct military confrontation in Europe and engaged in actual combat operations only to keep allies from defecting to the other side or to overthrow them after they had done so. Thus, the Soviet Union sent troops to preserve communist rule in East Germany (1953), Hungary (1956), Czechoslovakia (1968), and Afghanistan (1979). For its part, the United States helped overthrow a left-wing government in Guatemala (1954), supported an unsuccessful invasion of Cuba (1961), invaded the Dominican Republic (1965) and Grenada (1983), and undertook a long (1964–75) and unsuccessful effort to prevent communist North Vietnam from bringing South Vietnam under its rule.

In the course of the 1960s and '70s, however, the bipolar struggle between the Soviet and American blocs gave way to a more-complicated pattern of international relationships in which the world was no longer split into two clearly opposed blocs. A major split had occurred between the Soviet Union and China in 1960 and widened over the years, shattering the unity of the communist bloc. In the meantime, western Europe and Japan achieved dynamic economic growth in the 1950s and '60s, reducing their relative inferiority to the United States. Less-powerful countries had more room to assert their independence and often showed themselves resistant to superpower coercion or cajoling.

The 1970s saw an easing of Cold War tensions as evinced in the Strategic Arms Limitation Talks (SALT) that led to the SALT I and II agreements of 1972 and 1979, respectively, in which the two superpowers set limits on their antiballistic missiles and on their strategic missiles capable of carrying nuclear weapons. That was followed by a period of renewed Cold War tensions in the early 1980s as the two superpowers continued their massive arms buildup and competed for influence in the Third World.

But the Cold War began to break down in the late 1980s during the administration of Soviet leader Mikhail S. Gorbachev. He dismantled the totalitarian aspects of the Soviet system and began efforts to democratize the Soviet political system. When communist regimes in the Soviet-bloc countries of eastern Europe collapsed in 1989–90, Gorbachev acquiesced in their fall. The rise to power of democratic governments in East Germany, Poland, Hungary, and Czechoslovakia was quickly followed by the unification of West and East Germany under NATO auspices, again with Soviet approval.

Gorbachev's internal reforms had meanwhile weakened his own Communist Party and allowed power to shift to Russia and the other constituent republics of the Soviet Union. In

November 1989 the Berlin Wall fell, as East Germany opened its borders with West Germany and West Berlin. In late 1991 the Soviet Union collapsed and 15 newly independent nations were born from its corpse, including a Russia with a democratically elected, anticommunist leader. After almost half a century of distrust, marked by auxiliary conflicts around the globe, the Cold War had come to an end.

Historians have disagreed over whether the United States and the Soviet Union shared the blame for the amplification of tension between the two nations directly following World War II. As early as 1948 American left-liberals blamed the Harry S. Truman administration for the icy tone of its relations with Moscow, while rightists blamed the Communists but accused Franklin D. Roosevelt and Truman of appeasement. Moderates of both parties shared a consensus that Truman's containment policy was, as the historian Arthur Schlesinger, Jr., wrote, "the brave and essential response of free men to communist aggression." After all, Soviet premier Joseph Stalin's tyranny was undeniable, and his seizure of countries in eastern Europe one by one was reminiscent of Nazi German leader Adolf Hitler's "salami tactics." To be sure, Roosevelt may have helped to foster mistrust by refusing to discuss war aims earlier and then relying on vague principles, and Truman may have blundered or initiated steps that solidified the Cold War. Those steps, however, were taken only after substantial Soviet violation of wartime agreements and in fearful confusion over the motivations for Soviet policy. Was the U.S.S.R. implacably expansionist, or were its aims limited? Was it executing a plan based on Communist faith in world revolution, or reflecting the regime's need for foreign enemies to justify domestic terror, or merely pursuing the traditional aims of Russian imperialism? Or was it only Stalin's own paranoia or ambition that was responsible for Soviet aggression?

The fact that Western societies tended to parade their dis agreements and failures in public, in contrast to the Soviet fetish for secrecy, guaranteed that historical attention would fix on American motivations and mistakes. In the late 1950s and the 1960s, traditional left-liberal scholars smarting from the excesses of McCarthyism and new leftists of the Vietnam era began publishing revisionist interpretations of the origins of the Cold War. The "hard revisionism" of William Appleman Williams in 1959 depicted the Cold War in Marxist fashion as an episode in American economic expansion in which the U.S. government resorted to military threats to prevent Communists from closing off eastern European markets and raw materials to American corporations. Less rigidly ideological "soft revisionists" blamed the Cold War on the irascible Truman administration, which, they charged, had jettisoned the cooperative framework built up by Roosevelt at Tehrān and Yalta and had dropped the atomic bombs on Japan as a means of frightening the Russians and forcing an "American peace." These revisionist interpretations argued that Stalin could be excused for insisting on friendly governments on his borders after the Soviet Union had been brutally invaded and had lost 20,000,000 lives in the war. He was betrayed, said revisionists, by American militancy and Red-baiting after the death of Roosevelt.

Traditional historians countered that little evidence existed for most of the revisionist positions. To be sure, American hostility to Communism dated from 1917, but the record proved Roosevelt's commitment to good relations with Stalin, while no proof at all was forthcoming that American policy makers were anxious to penetrate eastern European markets, which were, in any case, of minor importance to the U.S. economy. The preponderance of evidence also indicated that the atomic decision was made for military considerations, although isolated advisers did hope that it would ease negotiations with Moscow. These and other examples led most historians to conclude that, while the revisionists brought to light new issues and exposed American aimlessness, inconsistency, and possible overreaction at the end of World War II, they failed to establish their primary theories of American guilt.

Historians with a longer perspective on the Cold War transcended the passions of Vietnam-era polarization and observed that deeper forces must have been at work for the Cold War to have persisted for so long after 1945. Indeed, it is difficult to imagine how leaders of the two countries could have sat down agreeably and settled the affairs of the world. The new superpowers were wrenched out of isolationism and thrust into roles of world leadership, they nurtured contrary universalist ideologies, and they mounted asymmetrical military threats (one based on conventional weapons, sheer numbers, and land power; the other on nuclear might, technological superiority, and air and sea power). To these liabilities could be added the fact that both countries had been forced into World War II by sneak attacks and had resolved never again to be seduced into appeasement or to be taken by surprise. This staunch resistance to appeasement, while preventing the outbreak of another worldwide hot war, led to a mutually destructive cold war that also proved to be global in scope.

CHAPTER 1

THE COLD WAR BEGINS IN EUROPE

The symbolic first meeting of American and Soviet soldiers occurred at Torgau, Ger., on April 25, 1945. Their handshakes and toasts in beer and vodka celebrated their common victory over Nazi Germany and marked the collapse of old Europe altogether; but their inarticulate grunts and exaggerated smiles presaged the lack of communication in their relationship to come. Grand wartime coalitions invariably break up once the common fight gives way to bickering over division of the spoils, but feuding victors after the wars of Louis XIV and Napoleon or World War I at least negotiated treaties of peace, while the rancour among them was moderated by time or the danger that the common enemy might rise again. After 1945, however, no grand peace conference convened, no common fear of Germany or Japan survived, and the quarrels among the victors only grew year by year into what the U.S. presidential adviser Bernard Baruch and the pundit Walter Lippmann termed a Cold War.

The U.S.–Soviet conflict began in 1945 over treatment of occupied Germany and the composition of the Polish government. It grew during 1946 as the Soviets communized the lands under their occupation and the victors failed to agree on a plan for the control of atomic energy. From 1947 to 1950 the reactions of Washington and Moscow to the perceived threats of the other solidified the division of Europe and much of the world into two blocs, and the Cold War became universalized, institutionalized, and militarized.

The settlement after World War II, therefore, was a peace without treaties, and the Cold War magnified, distorted, or otherwise played upon the other historical trends given impetus by the world wars of the 20th century: Asian nationalism, decolonization, the seeming culmination of the 37-year-old Chinese Revolution, the evolution of independent Communist parties in Yugoslavia and Asia, and western Europe's drive to end four centuries of conflict through economic integration. The early Cold War was not a decade of fear and failure alone but also a creative time that gave birth to the closest thing to a world order that had existed since 1914. With the sole major exception of the later Sino-Soviet split, the boundaries, institutions, and relationships fashioned in the late 1940s were very nearly the same ones that shaped world politics through the 1980s.

The World in 1945

Harry Truman had been an artilleryman in World War I and remembered well the lunar landscape of the Western Front. Yet, while driving from Potsdam to Berlin in July 1945, he exclaimed, "I never saw such destruction!" Almost all the great cities of central and eastern Europe were jagged with ruined buildings, pitted roads, wrecked bridges, and choked waterways. Amid it all were the gaunt survivors, perhaps 45,000,000 of them homeless, including 25,000,000 in those lands—Poland, the Ukraine, and Russia—that had been overrun and scorched two or three times. European communications and transportation reverted to 19th-century levels: 90 percent of French trucks and 82 percent of French locomotives were out of commission, as were over half the rolling stock in Germany and two-thirds of the Balkan railroads. European coal production was at 40 percent of prewar levels, and more than half the

continent's merchant marine no longer existed. Some 23 percent of Europe's farmland was out of production by war's end. Of course, people could be fed with American aid while the rubble was cleared away and utilities restored, but World War II cost Europe more in monetary terms than all its previous wars put together.

The war also set in motion the greatest *Völkerwanderung*—movement of peoples—since the barbarian incursions of the late Roman Empire. During the Nazi onslaught some 27,000,000 people fled or were forced out by war and persecution, and 4,500,000 more were seized for slave labour. When the Red Army advanced westward, millions more fled before it to escape reprisals or Communism. All told, about 60,000,000 people of 55 ethnic groups from 27 countries were uprooted. Finally, 7,000,000 Axis prisoners of war were in Allied hands, along with 8,000,000 Allied prisoners of war liberated from the Axis and 670,000 survivors of Nazi death camps.

The landscape in much of Japan was just as barren, its cities flattened by bombing, its industry and shipping destroyed. Large parts of China had been under foreign occupation for up to 14 years and—like Russia after World War I—still faced several years of destructive civil war. Indeed, World War II had laid waste every major industrial region of the globe except North America. The result was that in 1945–46 the United States accounted for almost half the gross world product of goods and services and enjoyed a technological lead symbolized by, but by no means limited to, its atomic monopoly. On the other hand, Americans as always wanted to demobilize rapidly and return to the private lives and careers interrupted by Pearl Harbor. The Soviet Union, by contrast, was in ruin, but its mighty armies occupied half a dozen states in the heart of Europe, while local Communist parties agitated in Italy and France. The United States and the Soviet Union thus appeared to pose asymmetrical threats to each other.

In fact, in the weeks after Germany's surrender, British prime minister Winston Churchill was so concerned about the Soviets taking over eastern Europe, in particular Poland, that he asked his military chiefs of staff to draw up plans for a join U.S.–British offensive against the Soviet Union. Codenamed Operation Unthinkable, in recognition of its unfeasibility, the plan would have required dozens of Allied divisions, and the Soviets were estimated to have twice as many men and tanks at their disposal. While nothing came of this proposal, it was a stark reminder of the tensions between the Soviets and the other Allies in the immediate aftermath of World War II.

U.S. Vision of Reconstruction

American planners envisioned postwar reconstruction in terms of Wilsonian internationalism but were determined to avoid the mistakes that resulted after 1918 in inflation, tariffs, debts, and reparations. In 1943 the United States sponsored the United Nations Relief and Rehabilitation Administration to distribute food and medicine to the stricken peoples in the war zones. At the Bretton Woods Conference in the summer of 1944 the United States presided over the creation of the International Monetary Fund (IMF) and the World Bank. After ratification by 29 countries, the Articles of Agreement drafted at Bretton Woods entered into force on December 27, 1945. The dollar was returned to gold convertibility at $35 per ounce and would serve as the world's reserve currency, while the pound, the franc, and other currencies were pegged to the dollar. Countries with temporary, moderate balance-of-payments deficits were expected to finance their deficits by borrowing foreign currencies from the IMF rather than by imposing exchange controls, devaluations, or deflationary economic policies that could spread their economic problems to other countries. The World Bank began operations in June 1946. Its first loans were geared toward the postwar reconstruction of western Europe.

Currency stability would permit the recovery of world trade, while a General Agreement on Tariffs and Trade (GATT), ratified in 1948, would ensure low tariffs and prevent a return to policies of economic nationalism. Rather, GATT promoted trade without discrimination, in which each member nation opened its markets equally to every other. Treasury Secretary Henry Morgenthau tried to entice the Soviets to join the Bretton Woods system, but the U.S.S.R. opted out of the new economic order.

THE CREATION AND MEMBERSHIP OF THE UN

Despite the problems encountered by the League of Nations in arbitrating conflict and ensuring international peace and security prior to World War II, the major Allied powers agreed during the war to establish a new global organization to help manage international affairs. The United States, the United Kingdom, and the Soviet Union took the lead in designing the new organization and determining its decision-making structure and functions.

Initially, the "Big Three" states and their respective leaders (Roosevelt, Churchill, and Stalin) were hindered by disagreements on issues that foreshadowed the Cold War. The Soviet Union demanded individual membership and voting rights for its constituent republics, and Britain wanted assurances that its colonies would not be placed under UN control. There also was disagreement over the voting system to be adopted in the Security Council, an issue that became famous as the "veto problem."

Proposals from previous conferences at Dumbarton Oaks and Yalta formed the basis of negotiations at the United Nations Conference on International Organization (UNCIO), which convened in San Francisco on April 25, 1945, and produced the final Charter of the United Nations. The San Francisco conference was attended by representatives of 50 countries from all geographic areas of the world. Many political issues were resolved by compromise, including the role of the organization in the promotion of economic and social welfare; the status of colonial areas and the distribution of trusteeships; the status of regional and defense arrangements; and Great Power dominance versus the equality of states. The UN Charter was unanimously adopted and signed on June 26 and promulgated on October 24, 1945.

Five countries—China, France, the Soviet Union (now Russia), the United Kingdom, and the United States—became permanent members of the Security Council, with the other ten seats on the council rotating on two-year terms among the other member nations. Given Cold War divisions between East and West, the requirement that the permanent members concur on the admission of new members at times posed serious obstacles. By 1950 only 9 of 31 applicants had been admitted to the organization. A package deal in 1955 resulted in the admission of 16 new states (4 eastern European communist states and 12 noncommunist countries).

The most contentious application for membership was that of the communist People's Republic of China, which was placed before the General Assembly and blocked by the United States at every session from 1950 to 1971. Finally, in 1971, the Assembly voted to admit the People's Republic and to expel the Republic of China (Taiwan). The People's Republic also received the Republic of China's permanent Security Council seat.

Controversy also arose over the issue of "divided" states. The two German states, the Federal Republic of Germany (West Germany) and the German Democratic Republic (East Germany), were admitted as members in 1973; these two seats were reduced to one after the country's reunification in October 1990. Vietnam was admitted in 1977, after the defeat of South Vietnam and the reunification of the country in 1975. North Korea and South Korea were admitted separately in 1991. That same year, upon the breakdown of the Soviet Union, Russia assumed the membership and permanent seat on the Security Council previously held by the Soviet Union.

Following worldwide decolonization from 1955 to 1960, 40 new members were admitted, and by the end of the 1970s there were about 150 members of the UN. Another significant increase occurred after 1989–90, when many former Soviet republics gained their independence. By 2015 the UN comprised more than 190 member states.

The American universalist program seemingly had more luck in the political realm. Roosevelt was convinced that the League of Nations had been doomed by the absence of the United States and the Soviet Union and thus was anxious to win Soviet participation in the compromises at Yalta. The Big Four powers accordingly drafted the Charter of the United Nations at the San Francisco Conference in April 1945. Roosevelt wisely appointed several leading Republicans to the U.S. delegation, avoiding Wilson's fatal error and securing the Senate ratification of the UN Charter on July 28, 1945, by a vote of 89–2. Like Wilson, Roosevelt and Truman hoped that future quarrels could be settled peacefully in the international body.

Postwar Conferences

By the time of the Potsdam Conference, Truman was already aware of Soviet unwillingness to permit representative governments and free elections in the countries under its control. The U.S.S.R. compelled the king of Romania to appoint a Communist-dominated government, Josip Broz Tito's Communists assumed control of a coalition with royalists in Yugoslavia, Communists dominated in Hungary and Bulgaria (where a reported 20,000 people were liquidated), and the Red Army extended an invitation to "consult" with 16 underground Polish leaders only to arrest them when they surfaced. As Stalin said to the Yugoslav Communist Milovan Djilas: "In this war each side imposes its system as far as its armies can reach. It cannot be otherwise."

On April 23, 1945, Truman scolded Soviet foreign minister Vyacheslav Mikhaylovic Molotov for these violations of the Yalta Accords and, when Molotov protested such undiplomatic conduct, replied, "Carry out your agreements and you won't get talked to like that." On May 11, three days after the German surrender, Truman abruptly ordered the termination of Lend-Lease aid to the U.S.S.R. Two weeks later Stalin replied in like terms to the envoy Harry Hopkins by way of protesting the suspension of Lend-Lease, Churchill's alleged plan to revive a *cordon sanitaire* on Russia's borders, and other matters. Hopkins, however, assured him of American goodwill and acquiesced in the imprisonment of the Polish leaders and the inclusion of only a few London Poles in the new government. The United States and Britain then recognized the Warsaw regime, assuring Soviet domination of Poland.

The short-lived détente was to be consummated at Potsdam, the last meeting among the Big Three, from July 17 to August 2, 1945. In the midst of the conference, however, the British electorate rejected Churchill at the polls, and the Labour Party leader Clement Attlee replaced him in the councils of the great. Aside from the Soviet promise to enter the war against Japan and Truman's hint that the United States had developed the atomic bomb, the Potsdam Conference dealt with postwar Europe. The U.S.S.R. was authorized to seize one-third of the German fleet, extract reparations-in-kind from its eastern German occupation zone, and benefit from a complicated formula for delivery of industrial goods from the western zones, 15 percent to be counted as payment for foodstuffs and other products sent from the Soviet zone. The conference provided for peace treaties with the defeated countries once they had "recognized democratic governments" and left their drafting to the Council of Foreign Ministers. Finally, the Potsdam nations agreed to prosecute Germans for war crimes in trials that were conducted at Nürnberg for a year after November 1945.

Potsdam, however, left the most divisive issues—the administration of Germany and the configuration of eastern European

Winston Churchill, Harry Truman, and Joseph Stalin during the Potsdam Conference.

governments—to future discussion. At the first such meeting, in September, the new U.S. secretary of state, James F. Byrnes, asked why Western newsmen were not allowed into eastern Europe and why governments could not be formed there that were democratic yet still friendly to Russia. Molotov asked on his own account why the U.S.S.R. was excluded from the administration of Japan.

Truman enumerated the principles of American foreign policy in his Navy Day speech of October 27. Its 12 points echoed the Fourteen Points of Woodrow Wilson, including national self-determination; nonrecognition of governments imposed by foreign powers; freedom of the seas, commerce, expression, and religion; and support for the United Nations. Confusion reigned in Washington, however, as to how to implement these principles in league with Moscow. As the political commentator James Reston observed, two schools of thought seemed to compete for the ear of the president. According to the first, Stalin was committed to limitless expansion and would only be encouraged by concessions. According to the second, Stalin was amenable to a structure of peace but could not be expected to loosen his hold on eastern Europe so long as the United States excluded him from, for instance, Japan. Truman and the State Department drifted between these two poles, searching for a key to unlock the secrets of the Kremlin and hence the appropriate U.S. policy.

Truman's last attempt to win the Soviets to his universalist vision was the Byrnes mission to Moscow in December 1945. There the Soviets promptly accepted an Anglo-American plan for a UN Atomic Energy Agency meant to control the development and use of nuclear power. Stalin also conceded that it might prove possible to make some changes in the Romanian and Bulgarian parliaments, though conceding nothing that might weaken his hold on the satellites. George F. Kennan of the U.S. embassy in Moscow called the concessions "fig leaves of democratic procedure to hide the nakedness of Stalinist dictatorship," while Truman's own dissatisfaction with the results at Moscow and growing domestic criticism of his "coddling" of the Russians were pushing him toward a drastic reformulation of policy.

The End of East–West Cooperation

Why, in fact, did Stalin engage in such a hurried takeover of eastern Europe when it was bound to provoke the United States (magnifying Soviet insecurity) and waste the opportunity for access to U.S. loans and perhaps even atomic secrets? Was not Stalin's policy, in retrospect, simply unwise? Such questions cannot be answered with assurance, since less is known about the postwar Stalinist era (1945–53) than any other in Soviet history, but the most tempting clue is again to be found in Stalin's domestic calculations. If the Soviet Union were to recover from the war, not to mention compete with the mighty United States, the population would have to be spurred to even greater efforts, which meant intensifying the campaign against alleged foreign threats.

What was more, the Soviets had only recently regained control of populations that had had contact with foreigners and, in some cases, collaborated with the invaders. Ukrainians in particular had tried to establish an autonomous status under the Nazis, and they persisted in guerrilla activity against the Soviets until 1947. If Soviet citizens were allowed widespread contact with foreigners through economic coop-eration, international institutions, and cultural exchanges, loyalty to the Communist regime might be weakened. Firm control of his eastern European neighbours helped assure Stalin of firm control at home. Indeed, he now ordered the utter isolation of Soviet life to the point that returning pris-oners of war were interned lest they "infect" their neighbours with notions of the outside world. Perhaps Stalin did not really fear an attack from the "imperialists" or consider a Soviet invasion of western Europe, but neither could he wel-come the Americans and British as genuine comrades in peace without undermining the ideology and the emergency that justified his own iron rule.

A swift return to Communist orthodoxy accompanied the clampdown on foreign contacts. During the war the U.S.S.R.'s leading economist, Evgeny Varga of the Institute of World

Economy and World Politics, argued that government controls in the United States had moderated the influence of monopolies, permitting both dynamic growth and a mellower foreign policy. The U.S.S.R. might therefore benefit from East–West cooperation and prevent the division of the world into economic blocs. Stalin appeared to tolerate this nontraditionalist view as long as large loans from the United States and the World Bank were a possibility. But the suspension of Lend-Lease, opposition to a Soviet loan in the State Department, and Stalin's renewed rejection of consumerism doomed these moderate views on the world economy.

The new Five-Year Plan, announced at the start of 1946, called for continued concentration on heavy industry and military technology. The war and victory, said Stalin, had justified his harsh policies of the 1930s, and he called on Soviet scientists to overtake and surpass Western science. Soviet economists perforce embraced the traditional view that Western economies were about to enter a new period of inflation and unemployment that would increase the imperialist pressure for war. Andrey Zhdanov, the Communist leader of Leningrad, was a bellwether. In 1945 he wanted to reward the Soviet people with consumer goods for their wartime sacrifices; in early 1947 he espoused the theory of the "two camps," the peace-loving, progressive camp led by the Soviet Union and the militaristic, reactionary camp led by the United States.

American confusion came to an end after Feb. 9, 1946, when Stalin's great speech inaugurating the Five-Year Plan reiterated clearly his implacable hostility to the West. Kennan responded with his famous "Long Telegram" from Moscow (February 22), which for years to come served as a primer on Soviet behaviour for many in Washington. The Kremlin's "neurotic view of world affairs," he wrote, was the product of centuries of Russian isolation and insecurity vis-à-vis the more advanced West. The Soviets, like the tsars, viewed the influx of Western ideas as the greatest threat to their continued power, and they clung to Marxist ideology as a cover for their disregard for "every single ethical value in their methods and tactics." The U.S.S.R. was not Nazi Germany—it would not seek war and was averse to risk taking—but it would employ every means of subverting, dividing, and undermining the West through the actions of Communists and fellow travelers. Kennan's advice was to expect nothing from negotiations but to remain confident and healthy, lest the United States become like those with whom it was contending.

Kennan's analysis implied several important conclusions: that the Wilsonian vision inherited from Roosevelt was fruitless; that the United States must take the lead in organizing the Western world; that the Truman administration must prevent a renewal of isolationism and persuade the American people to shoulder their new responsibilities. Churchill, though out of office, aided this agenda when he warned the American people (with Truman's confidential endorsement) from Fulton, Mo., on March 5, 1946, that an "iron curtain" had descended across the European continent.

Peace Treaties and Territorial Agreements

The early spring of 1946 was a turning point when the United States gave up its hopes of cooperation in favour of what would soon be called "containment." The first manifestation occurred in March 1946, when the U.S.S.R. failed to evacuate Iran on schedule and Secretary of State Byrnes was obliged to go to the UN Security Council and even hint at hostilities to get Moscow to retreat. This incident, together with Soviet pressure on Turkey and Yugoslav involvement in the Greek civil war, seemed to indicate that Communists were prepared to use force to expand.

The year 1946 saw many meetings of the Council of Foreign Ministers, which ultimately produced treaties of peace with Italy, Hungary, Romania, Finland, and Bulgaria, signed on Feb. 10, 1947. Border questions after World War II were comparatively minor—a somewhat ironic fact, given the interwar attacks on Versailles by all parties. Romania ceded northern Bukovina and Bessarabia back to the U.S.S.R., which also claimed Petsamo and the Karelian Isthmus from Finland and the Carpatho-Ukraine region from Czechoslovakia. Hungary returned northern Transylvania to Romania. Italy ceded the Dodecanese islands to Greece and surrendered its overseas colonies, although a Soviet demand for a trusteeship over Libya was denied. Trieste was contested by Italy and Yugoslavia and remained under Western occupation until 1954. The major change affected Poland, which was figuratively picked up and moved some 150 miles to the west. This meant that large portions of eastern Germany came under Polish administration, while the U.S.S.R. absorbed the entire Baltic coast as far as the venerable German port of Königsberg (Kaliningrad). The U.S.S.R. was the only power to make significant territorial gains from the war.

Four-power cooperation in Germany continued to deteriorate. The Americans had agreed at Potsdam to reparations-in-kind but opposed extreme efforts by the Soviets and the French to pauperize the Germans lest the burden of feeding them fall entirely on the American taxpayer. What was more, the Soviets would be unwilling (in Kennan's view) to countenance centralized German institutions unless they were in a position to use them to communize the entire country. In early May 1946, General Lucius Clay, commanding the U.S. zone, refused to authorize shipments out of western Germany until agreement was reached on treating Germany as a unit under four-power control. On September 6, Byrnes then announced a new policy: if unification of all Germany proved impossible, the United States would instead promote "maximum possible unification" (*i.e.,* in the western zones only). This ensured that Germany would remain divided long afterward.

Atomic Energy

The superpowers also failed to join hands on atomic energy. Despite resistance from powerful circles in the press, Congress, and the military against any giveaway of atomic secrets, Byrnes appointed a committee in January 1946 to draft proposals for international control of atomic energy. The resulting (Dean) Acheson–(David) Lilienthal Report called for a UN authority to survey and control all uranium deposits and ensure that atomic research was conducted for peaceful purposes only. Once controls were in place, the United States would relinquish its arsenal and scientific information to the world community. Truman entrusted the diplomatic task to Baruch, who insisted that nations not be allowed to employ their Security Council veto in atomic matters. He then appealed to the UN on June 14, 1946: "We are here to make a choice between the quick and the dead."

The Soviet plan, presented by Andrey Gromyko, called instead for immediate prohibition of all manufacture and use of atomic weapons. Measures to ensure compliance would follow, but there could be no tampering with the Security Council veto. Western delegates pointed out that the Soviets were asking the United States to give up its monopoly and make public all its data in return for a paper promise of compliance. Gromyko countered that the United States was asking all other countries to reveal the state of their own research before it gave up its own arsenal. At the final vote in December, the

U.S.S.R. and Poland vetoed the Baruch Plan, and international control of atomic energy ceased to be a possibility. While the United States was not as forthcoming as it might have been, the Soviet refusal to allow on-site inspection would frustrate disarmament for the next 40 years.

The Marshall Plan

By the turn of 1947 it appeared that Truman's foreign policy was foundering. His secretary of agriculture, Henry A. Wallace, had been outspoken in criticism of the Baruch Plan and of the policy of "getting tough" with the Soviets. Upon resigning he became a leader of those whom Truman privately described as the "Reds, phonies and the parlour pinks" that he feared were "a sabotage front for Uncle Joe Stalin." The 1946 elections then returned a Republican Congress bent on cutting costs and "bringing the boys home." Yet the United States was on the verge of the greatest reversal of its foreign policy traditions since 1917.

On Feb. 21, 1947, the British government announced that its economic difficulties would force it to suspend economic and military aid to Greece and Turkey by March 31. Greece was embroiled in civil war provoked by Communists. Turkey was under Soviet pressure for bases and naval passage through the Dardanelles. If those countries succumbed to Communist influence, the Mediterranean and the entire Middle East might follow. Truman, his new secretary of state, George C. Marshall, and Marshall's deputy, Dean Acheson, resolved at once that the United States must step in. On February 27 Acheson impressed congressional leaders with a vivid account of the Soviet strategy of expansion and its implications for American security. After a tense silence, Republican Senator Arthur Vandenberg vowed to support the new policy if Truman would explain it with equal clarity to the American people. On March 12, Truman accordingly told Congress that "at the present moment in world history nearly every nation must choose between alternative ways of life. The choice is too often not a free one. . . . It must be the policy of the United States to support free people who are resisting attempted subjugation by armed minorities or by outside pressure." He asked for $400,000,000 in aid specifically for Greece and Turkey, but the Truman Doctrine thus propounded universalized the American commitment to contain the spread of Communism.

The mobilization of American might for this task followed swiftly. On June 5, 1947, at Harvard University, Marshall called for a massive program of foreign aid to help the European states recover. In July, Kennan, signing himself "X," educated the public on "The Sources of Soviet Conduct" and outlined the strategy of containment in the journal *Foreign Affairs*. The National Military Establishment Act of 1947 (in the works since the war) created a permanent Joint Chiefs of Staff, a single secretary of defense, the U.S. Air Force as a separate service with its nuclear-armed Strategic Air Command, and the Central Intelligence Agency (CIA). Kennan himself soon criticized the Truman Doctrine as indiscriminate and excessively military. Drawing on classical geopolitics, he narrowed U.S. interests to the protection of those industrial regions not yet in the hands of the Soviet Union (North America, Britain, Germany, and Japan). In practice, however, defense of those regions seemed to require defense of contiguous areas as well. Japanese security, for instance, depended on the fate of Korea, and European security on not being outflanked in the Middle East. American responsibilities, therefore, could easily appear to be global.

The Marshall Plan was born in the State Department in response to the fact that western Europe was making little progress toward prosperity and stability. Britain was exhausted and committed to the Labour government's extensive welfare programs. In France, Charles de Gaulle's postwar government quickly gave way to a Fourth Republic paralyzed by quarreling factions that included a large, disciplined Communist party. In Italy, too, Communists threatened to gain power by parliamentary means. All suffered from underproduction, a shortage of capital, and energy shortages exacerbated by the severe winter of 1946–47. Marshall therefore put forward a plan for cash grants to a joint European economic council "to assist in the return of normal economic health, without which there can be no political stability and no assured peace."

The British foreign secretary, Ernest Bevin, spoke for western Europe when he told Parliament, "When the Marshall proposals were announced, I grabbed them with both hands." At Kennan's insistence, Marshall aid was offered to all of Europe, including the Soviet bloc, but Stalin denounced the plan as a capitalist plot. The one eastern European state not yet communized, Czechoslovakia, attempted to join the Marshall Plan, but Communist pressure forced it to back out. In February 1948, less than 10 years after Munich, the Czech Communist party subverted the republic and Czech democracy again fell to totalitarian rule, a tragedy punctuated by the suicide—or murder—of Foreign Minister Jan Masaryk. Stalin reinforced his attack on the Marshall Plan by reviving the Communist International, now called the Communist Information Bureau (Cominform), in October 1947 and by escalating ideological warfare against the West.

The new hope kindled in western Europe by the Marshall Plan helped secure the defeat of the Communists in the 1948 Italian election (the $1,000,000 of CIA funds for the Christian Democrats was hardly decisive) and stabilize politics elsewhere in western Europe. Under the Marshall Plan, the United States then transferred $13,600,000,000 to the stricken economies of western Europe in addition to $9,500,000,000 in earlier loans and $500,000,000 in private charity.

The Berlin Blockade and Airlift

The Marshall Plan's manifold effects included the hardening of the division of Europe, the movement for integration within western Europe, and the creation of the two Germanies. "Bizonia," the product of an economic merger between the U.S. and British occupation zones, was announced on May 29, 1947, and a new U.S. policy followed on July 11 that ended Germany's punitive period and aimed at making its economy self-sufficient. In March 1948 some of the western European states responded to the coup in Czechoslovakia by signing the Brussels Treaty, creating a collective defense alliance. The Allied powers (the United States, the United Kingdom, and France) also decided to unite their different occupation zones of Germany and establish a single West German currency and government. In response, the Soviets walked out of the Allied Control Council. The new deutsche mark was introduced in West Berlin (as throughout West Germany), which the Soviets regarded as a violation of agreements with the Allies.

On June 24, Soviet occupation forces in the eastern zone blocked Allied road, rail, and water access to the western zones of Berlin. They declared that the four-power administration of Berlin had ceased and that the Allies no longer had any rights there. This first Berlin crisis, made possible by the anomaly of a U.S.-British-French interest 100 miles inside the Soviet zone, forced Truman to define the limits of his "get tough" policy. Clay and Acheson advocated sending an armed convoy along the access routes to assert Allied rights, but neither the Joint Chiefs nor the British and French were prepared to risk war. Instead, the United States and Britain responded with an

A U.S. C-47 cargo plane approaches Berlin in 1948 with much-needed relief supplies for the citizens of West Berlin.

enormous airlift, totalling 277,264 sorties, to keep western Berlin supplied with food, fuel, and medicine. They also organized a similar "airlift" in the opposite direction of West Berlin's greatly reduced industrial exports. By mid-July the Soviet army of occupation in East Germany had increased to 40 divisions, against 8 in the Allied sectors. By the end of July three groups of U.S. strategic bombers had been sent as reinforcements to Britain. Tension remained high, but war did not break out.

Perhaps Stalin hoped to drive the Allies from Berlin, or to prevent the setting up and possible rearmament of a West German state, or to induce the American electorate in 1948 to return to isolationism. In the event, the blockade only frightened the Western powers into stronger new measures.

Despite dire shortages of fuel and electricity, the airlift kept life going in West Berlin for 11 months, until on May 12, 1949, the Soviet Union lifted the blockade. The airlift continued until September 30, at a total cost of $224 million and after delivery of 2,323,738 tons of food, fuel, machinery, and other supplies. The end to the blockade was brought about because of countermeasures imposed by the Allies on East German communications and, above all, because of the Western embargo placed on all strategic exports from the Eastern bloc. As a result of the blockade and airlift, Berlin became a symbol of the Allies' willingness to oppose further Soviet expansion in Europe.

On April 4, 1949, the foreign ministers of the United States, Britain, France, Belgium, the Netherlands, Luxembourg, Italy, Portugal, Denmark, Iceland, Norway, and Canada founded the North Atlantic Treaty Organization (NATO) in Washington, D.C., providing for mutual aid in case of attack against any member. On May 8, the West German parliamentary council adopted a constitution, and on May 23 the Federal Republic of Germany came into being. The Soviets countered by creating mirror institutions—the German Democratic Republic (Oct. 7, 1949) and the Council for Mutual Economic Assistance (Comecon) in the Soviet bloc.

Assumptions Debunked

The parallel and hostile German states and regional alliances institutionalized and militarized the Cold War even as the Communist ideological offensive and the Truman Doctrine had universalized it. Before this first phase of the Cold War closed, however, two events called into question root assumptions of the two sides. The first was the West's assumption that Communism was a monolithic movement controlled from the Kremlin. In June 1948 the world became aware of a rift between Stalin and Tito that threatened to shake the Soviet empire of "people's democracies." This rift could be traced to the war, in which Tito's Communist partisans had expelled the Nazis from Yugoslavia without large-scale aid from the Soviet Union. As a national hero, Tito had strong domestic support and thus was not personally dependent on Stalin. He even persevered in support for the Greek Communists while Stalin was adhering to his 1944 agreement with Churchill to keep hands off Greece. When Stalin and Molotov vetoed his plans for a Balkan confederation, Tito purged Yugoslav Communists known to be in the pay of Moscow. Stalin countered with brutal threats and a purge of Communists in the satellites accused of Titoist tendencies. But Tito held firm: Yugoslavia would "choose its own path to Socialism," seek economic ties with the West, and indirectly place itself under Western protection. Tito also ceased to support the Greek Communists, and the civil war there soon ended in a victory for the royal government (October 1949). In the ensuing war of words, economic boycotts, and occasional armed provocations (during which Stalin briefly considered military intervention), Yugoslavia was cut off from the Soviet Union and its eastern European satellites and steadily drew closer to the West.

The second assumption of the early Cold War was shattered in August 1949 when the Soviet Union exploded its first atomic bomb. Its development might have been hastened by espionage, but Soviets had been among the leaders in nuclear physics before the war, and knowledgeable observers had known that a Soviet atomic bomb was only a matter of time.

The Nature and Role of Germany

The shared horror of World War II and the decline of Europe from the seat of world power into an arena of U.S.–Soviet competition revived the ancient dream of European unity. In modern times, Roman Catholics, liberals, and Socialists had all conceived of one means or another to transcend nationalism, and after 1945 a combination of factors made the dream plausible. First, the Soviet threat gave western Europeans an incentive to unite for defense and economic recovery. Second, the very scale of the superpowers suggested that Europeans must pool their resources if they hoped to play a major role in world affairs. Third, two world wars and the Fascist interlude had discredited nationalism and propelled moderate Christian Democrats and Social Democrats to prominence in postwar Europe. Fourth, integration was a means by which German economic and military power might be safely revived. Fifth, centralized planning, which had evolved naturally with the war economies, made economic integration seem possible and attractive. Finally, the United States used its leverage through the Marshall Plan to encourage multinational institutions, cooperation, and free trade.

In early disputes over the occupation of Germany, France often sided with the U.S.S.R. in order to keep Germany weak and obtain reparations. The Berlin crisis of 1948, however, convinced the French that a way must be found to reconcile German recovery with their own security. The architects of an integrationist solution were the French technocrat Jean Monnet and Foreign Minister Robert Schuman. The Schuman Plan of May 1950 called for a merger of the western European coal and steel industries to hasten recovery, forestall competition, and make future wars between France and Germany impossible.

The patriarchal chancellor of the new West German republic, Konrad Adenauer, embraced the offer at once, for the primary foreign policy goal of his new state was economic and political rehabilitation. The founding of the West German state was his first success; the drafting of a sturdy democratic constitution was the second; his adoption, with Ludwig Erhard, of a dynamic free-market economic policy was the third. Once Marshall Plan aid arrived, West Germany was well on its way to *Wirtschaftswunder,* the economic miracle of the 1950s, but it remained for Adenauer to achieve security and full sovereign rights for West Germany. The Cold War permitted him to do both at once. By moving West Germany into the democratic free-market camp he earned protection and trust from the West.

Of course, Adenauer could not ignore the emotional issue of German reunification, and thus he refused to recognize the East German regime or Polish control of the lands east of the Oder-Neisse rivers. The Hallstein Doctrine extended this non-recognition to all countries that recognized East Germany. Adenauer knew, however, that to base policy on the prospect of reunification was unrealistic. The Soviets' Prague Proposals of October 1950 had envisioned a united, demilitarized German state—Kennan now endorsed such a neutral zone in central Europe to separate the Cold War rivals—but the Soviets insisted on a Constituent Council with equal representation for East and West Germany, even though the West had twice the population. At best, the East German delegation could block progress indefinitely while preventing West Germany from joining the Western bloc. At worst, the Soviets might subvert or coerce a disarmed Germany into alignment with Moscow. In the atmosphere of the Korean War, the Prague Proposals could not be taken up with confidence.

Instead, Adenauer endorsed the Schuman Plan and helped to found the European Coal and Steel Community among "the Six": France, West Germany, Italy, Belgium, the Netherlands, and Luxembourg. The Korean War sparked the next initiative toward integration when the United States, bogged down in Asia, requested a sizable increase in the European contribution to NATO. In 1951 the French and British cabinets both fell over the costly issue of rearmament before a committee managed to work out an acceptable distribution of burdens in October. The obvious solution was German rearmament, something the nervous French refused to countenance unless the German army were merged into an international force, a European Defense Community (EDC). The implications were profound, for a common western European army would require a common defense ministry, coordinated foreign policy, a joint defense budget, even a common parliament to approve spending and policy.

In sum, the EDC would go far toward creating a United States of Europe. The West German parliament was first to ratify the EDC, in March 1953, but Britain, still clinging to the vestiges of empire and its "special relationship" with the United States, opted out. As Anthony Eden put it, joining a European federation "is something which we know, in our bones, we cannot do." The French, in turn, debated the issue until Stalin's death and the Korean armistice eroded the sense of emergency. French Communists, of course, opposed the EDC, while Gaullists blanched at merging France's proud services into a European potpourri. Despite Dulles' threat of an "agonizing reappraisal" of U.S. policy should the EDC fail, the French parliament voted it down on Aug. 30, 1954. An alternate solution quickly followed: West Germany was simply admitted to NATO and its *Bundeswehr* (armed forces) placed under Allied command. The Soviets responded in 1955 by creating the Warsaw Pact, a military alliance of the U.S.S.R. and its eastern European satellites.

Postwar European Recovery

The first postwar decade was one of anxiety and crisis for Europe but one also of astounding economic recovery. Thanks to rational planning, labour–management cooperation, emphasis on production, the Marshall Plan, and the very destructiveness of the war, which made new plant construction necessary and thorough, the members of the Organisation for European Economic Co-operation all exceeded their prewar production levels by 1950 and achieved an annual average growth rate of 5 to 6 percent through 1955. The political stability wrought by the Cold War and the Western alliance and by the American military umbrella, which permitted western Europeans to devote more resources to building the welfare state, made for unprecedented prosperity.

Eastern Europe also recovered from the war, but more slowly and not always to its own benefit. In the late 1940s the U.S.S.R. forced one-sided trade treaties on its satellites so that Polish and Romanian foodstuffs and Czechoslovakian and East German technology flowed to the U.S.S.R. rather than to world

A demonstration against Soviet intervention in Budapest on October 23, 1956.

markets. Stalin's death on March 5, 1953, sparked hopes for a thaw in the eastern bloc and in the Cold War. The ephemeral collective leadership that succeeded him executed the hated secret-police chief, Lavrenty Beria, and released thousands from prison camps. Riots in East Germany and Poland also induced Moscow to scale back its exploitation of the satellites and to reduce reparations from East Germany. A Soviet delegation even visited Belgrade in 1955 to attempt a reconciliation with Tito. That same year the Austrian State Treaty provided for the first Soviet military withdrawal since the war and brought into being a neutral Austrian state.

In 1956 Nikita Khrushchev emerged as the new Soviet premier and shocked the 20th Party Congress with his midnight speech denouncing Stalin's "cult of personality" and manifold crimes against the party. De-Stalinization, however, even though carefully undertaken, created a crisis of legitimacy for the Soviet empire. In the summer of 1956 Władisław Gomułka rose to leadership of the Polish Communist Party on a wave of strikes and riots. When Moscow received his reassurances and allowed him to stay in power, other eastern Europeans were tempted to test the limits of de-Stalinization. Encouraged by the new freedom of debate and criticism, a rising tide of unrest and discontent in Hungary broke out into active fighting in October 1956. Rebels won the first phase of the revolution, and Imre Nagy became premier, agreeing to establish a multiparty system. He also released the Roman Catholic primate József

Cardinal Mindszenty from his long imprisonment and promised freedom of speech and the withdrawal of Hungary from the Warsaw Pact. On Nov. 1, 1956, he declared Hungarian neutrality and appealed to the United Nations for support, but Western powers were reluctant to risk a global confrontation. On Nov. 4, 1956, the Soviet Union invaded Hungary to stop the revolution, and Nagy was executed for treason in 1958. Nevertheless, Stalinist-type domination and exploitation did not return, and Hungary thereafter experienced a slow evolution toward some internal autonomy.

CHAPTER 2

THE COLD WAR IN ASIA AND THE MIDDLE EAST

E urope was far from the only front of the Cold War in the late 1940s and 1950s. Clashes across Asia and the Middle East contributed to and exacerbated the tension. For seven years after Japan's unconditional surrender to the Allies, the nation was under military occupation by the United States, to the chagrin of Soviet officials who believed they should be more involved. Meanwhile, the Chinese Civil War, which had begun in the mid-1920s, intensified again; in 1949 the Communists declared victory, proclaiming the People's Republic of China. Similar to Germany, Korea was effectively divided into U.S. and Soviet occupation zones that soon became separate governments; unlike in Germany, this situation devolved into war that ended with a demilitarized zone between the two states along the 38th parallel, which had been roughly the prewar boundary. In the Middle East, the declaration of the Jewish state of Israel triggered the first of many Arab-Israeli wars, while Egypt wrested control of the Suez Canal from British and French interests. Also during this era, the arms race between the United States and the Soviet Union reached a new frontier as both sides began developing satellites, culminating in the Soviet launch of Sputnik 1 on Oct. 4, 1957. With all of these conflicts around the world serving as proxy wars for the Cold War's two main adversaries, it was clear that tension between the two superpowers would continue into the 1960s.

U.S. Occupation of Japan

From 1945 to 1952 Japan was under Allied military occupation, headed by the Supreme Commander for Allied Powers (SCAP), a position held by U.S. General Douglas MacArthur until 1951. Although nominally directed by a multinational Far Eastern Commission in Washington, D.C., and an Allied Council in Tokyo—which included the United States, the Soviet Union, China, and the Commonwealth countries—the occupation was almost entirely an American affair. While MacArthur developed a large General Headquarters in Tokyo to carry out occupation policy, supported by local "military government" teams, Japan, unlike Germany, was not governed directly by foreign troops. Instead, SCAP relied on the Japanese government and its organs, particularly the bureaucracy, to carry out its directives.

The occupation, like the Taika Reform of the 7th century and the Meiji Restoration 80 years earlier, represented a period of rapid social and institutional change that was based on the borrowing and incorporation of foreign models. General principles for the proposed governance of Japan had been spelled out in the Potsdam Declaration and elucidated in U.S. government policy statements drawn up and for-warded to MacArthur in August 1945. The essence of these policies was simple and straightforward: the demilitarization of Japan, so that it would not again become a danger to peace; democratization, meaning that, while no particular form of government would be forced upon the Japanese, efforts would be made to develop a political system under which individual rights would be guaranteed and protected; and the establishment of an economy that could adequately support a peaceful and democratic Japan.

MacArthur himself shared the vision of a demilitarized and democratic Japan and was well suited to the task at hand. An administrator of considerable skill, he possessed elements of leadership and charisma that appealed to the defeated Japanese. Brooking neither domestic nor foreign interference, MacArthur enthusiastically set about creating a new Japan. He encouraged an environment in which new forces could and did rise, and, where his reforms corresponded to trends already established in Japanese society, they played a vital role in Japan's recovery as a free and independent nation.

In the early months of the occupation, SCAP acted swiftly to remove the principal supports of the militarist state. The armed forces were demobilized and millions of Japanese troops and civilians abroad repatriated. The empire was disbanded. State Shintō was disestablished, and nationalist organizations were abolished and their members removed from important posts. Japan's armament industries were dismantled. The Home Ministry with its prewar powers over the police and local government was abolished; the police force was decentralized and its extensive power revoked. The Education Ministry's sweeping powers over education were curtailed, and compulsory courses on ethics (*shūshin*) were eliminated. All individuals prominent in wartime organizations and politics, including commissioned officers of the armed services and all high executives of the principal industrial firms, were removed from their positions. An international tribunal was established to conduct war crimes trials, and seven men, including the wartime prime minister Tōjō, were convicted and hanged; another 16 were sentenced to life imprisonment. Other reforms included restoring civil rights, universal suffrage, and parliamentary government, encouraging labour unions, and emancipating women.

In the 1947 constitution drafted by MacArthur's staff Japan renounced war and limited its military to a token force. The

The courtroom where Tōjō Hideki was tried and convicted of war crimes in 1946.

emphasis in the new constitution was clearly on the people rather than the throne. Sovereignty now lay with the people, and the emperor, no longer "sacred" or "inviolable," was now described as the "symbol of the state and of the unity of the people." Despite its hasty preparation and foreign inspiration, the new constitution gained wide public support. During the Korean War a majority of the Allies signed a separate peace treaty and the United States entered into a mutual security pact with Japan (Sept. 8, 1951). These policies laid the foundation for a peaceful and prosperous Japan, and the occupation of Japan ended on April 28, 1952, but the United States took upon itself the burden of defending the western Pacific for the foreseeable future.

The Creation of Israel

Islāmic and South Asian nationalism, first awakened in the era of the first World War, triumphed in the wake of the second, bringing on in the years 1946–50 the first great wave of decolonization. The British and French fulfilled their wartime promises by evacuating and recognizing the sovereignty of Egypt, Jordan, Lebanon, and Syria in 1946 and Iraq in 1947. (Oman and Yemen remained under British administration until the 1960s, Kuwait and the Trucial States [United Arab Emirates] until 1971.) The strategic importance of the Middle East derived from its vast oil reserves, the Suez Canal, and its position on the southern rim of the U.S.S.R. While the Islāmic kingdoms and republics were not drawn to Communist ideology, the Soviets hoped to expand their influence by pressuring Turkey and Iran and involving themselves in the intramural quarrels of the region. Chief among these was the Arab-Israeli dispute.

The Zionist movement of the late 19th century had led by 1917 to the Balfour Declaration, by which Britain promised an eventual homeland for Jews in Palestine. When that former Ottoman province became a British mandate under the League of Nations in 1922, it contained about 700,000 people, of whom only 58,000 were Jews. By the end of the 1920s, however, the Jewish community had tripled, and, with the encouragement of Amīn al-Ḥusaynī, grand mufti of Jerusalem and admirer of the Nazis, Arab resentment exploded in bloody riots in 1929 and again in 1936–39. For self-protection the Jews formed Haganah (Defense), an underground militia that by 1939 had grown into a semiprofessional army. The Zionist cause then began to benefit from the worldwide sympathy caused by the Nazi Holocaust and by Haganah cobelligerency in the British war against Germany. The Irgun Zvai Leumi (National Military Organization), a Zionist terror organization under Menachem Begin, and the Abraham Stern Group, which found even the Irgun too mild, turned against the British occupation in 1944 despite vehement opposition from Chaim Weizmann and others promoting the Jewish cause overseas. The newly formed Arab League, in turn, pledged in March 1945 to prevent the formation of any Jewish state in Palestine.

Meanwhile, Zionists concentrated on the United States, whose large Jewish voting bloc was believed likely to influence policy. In the 1944 campaign Roosevelt endorsed the founding of a "free and democratic Jewish Commonwealth," and U.S. policy subsequently clashed with Britain's, which aimed at maintaining paramountcy in the region through good relations with the Arabs. Foreign Secretary Bevin opposed and Truman endorsed a proposal in April 1946 by an Anglo-American Committee of Inquiry to allow another 100,000 Jews into Palestine, an idea dwarfed by David Ben-Gurion's demand for 1,200,000. Jewish terrorism exacerbated British hostility through such incidents as the flogging and murder of British soldiers, culminating in the bombing of the King David Hotel on July 22, 1946, in which 41 Arabs, 28 British, and 22 others died. All told, Jewish terrorists killed 127 British soldiers and wounded 331 from 1944 to 1948, as well as thousands of Arabs. On the other hand, heartrending tales of Jewish survivors of Nazi Europe being turned back from their "promised land" also tugged at Western consciences.

On April 2, 1947, Bevin washed his hands of Palestine and placed it on the docket of the UN, which recommended partition into Jewish and Arab states. The United States and Britain feared that the Arabs would turn to the Soviets for aid, but the

U.S.S.R. mystified all parties in October by agreeing with the American plan for partition. The Soviets apparently hoped to hasten British withdrawal, insinuate themselves into Middle Eastern diplomacy, and profit from the discord following partition. The General Assembly approved partition on November 29, granting to Jews some 5,500 square miles, mostly in the arid Negev. When the Arab League proclaimed a jihad (holy war) against the Jews, Truman's advisers began to reconsider partition, for the loss of Arab oil might cripple the Marshall Plan and the U.S. military in case of war. When, however, the British pulled out and Ben-Gurion declared the state of Israel on May 14, 1948, Stalin and Truman (whether out of sympathy or domestic politics) immediately advanced recognition.

At the moment of partition the number of Jews had risen to some 35 percent of the total population of Palestine, and they were faced with Arab League forces totaling 40,000 men. The Haganah fielded about 30,000 volunteers armed with Czechoslovakian weapons sent at the behest of the U.S.S.R. On the day after partition the Arab League launched its attack, but the desperate Jewish defense prevailed on all five fronts. The UN called for a cease-fire on May 20 and appointed Folke, Count Bernadotte, as mediator, but his new partition plan was unacceptable to both sides. A 10-day Israeli offensive in July destroyed the Arab armies as an offensive force, at the cost of 838 Israeli lives. Members of the Stern Group assassinated Bernadotte on September 17. A final offensive in October carried the Israelis to the Lebanese border and the edge of the Golan Heights in the north and to the Gulf of Aqaba and into the Sinai in the south. Armistice talks resumed on Rhodes on Jan. 13, 1949, with the American Ralph Bunche mediating, and a truce followed in March. No Arab state recognized Israel's legitimacy, however. More than a half-million Palestinian refugees were scattered around the Arab world. Between 1948 and 1957 some 567,000 Jews were expelled from Arab states, nearly all of whom resettled in Israel. The 1948 war thus marked only the beginning of trouble in the region.

South Asia

The British faced a similar problem on a much larger scale in India, whose population included 250,000,000 Hindus, 90,000,000 Muslims, and 60,000,000 distributed among various ethnic and religious minorities. Between the wars Mohandas Gandhi's passive-resistance campaigns had crystallized Indian nationalism, which was nurtured in part by the relative leniency of British rule. Parliament set in motion the process leading to home rule in 1935, and the Attlee Cabinet rewarded India for its wartime loyalty by instructing Lord Mountbatten on Feb. 20, 1947, to prepare India for independence by June 1948. He did so, too hastily, in only six months, and the partition of the subcontinent into a mainly Hindu India and a mainly Muslim but divided Pakistan (including part of Bengal in the east) at midnight on Aug. 14–15, 1947, was accompanied by panicky flight and riots between Hindus and Muslims that claimed between 200,000 and 600,000 lives. Perhaps a bloodbath was inevitable whatever Mountbatten did or however long he took to do it. Nothing, however, tarnished Britain's colonial record in India so much as its termination. The Congress Party of Jawaharlal Nehru then took firm control and governed the Dominion (after 1950 the Republic) of India in parliamentary style and made India one of the first decolonized states to adopt a posture of nonalignment among the great powers. Disputes with Pakistan, especially over the contested province of Jammu and Kashmir, however, ensured continued strife on the subcontinent.

Elsewhere in South Asia the colonial powers expelled the Japanese only to confront indigenous nationalist forces.

The British fought a successful counterinsurgency against Communist guerrillas in Malaya, but the French waged a protracted and ultimately unsuccessful war with the Communist Viet Minh in Indochina, while the Dutch failed to subdue nationalists in Indonesia and granted independence in 1949. The United States transferred power peacefully in the Philippines; the Republic of the Philippines was proclaimed on July 4, 1946.

The Chinese Civil War

The Asian future would be determined above all by the outcome of the civil war in China, a war that had never totally ceased even during the Japanese invasion and occupation. In 1945, Truman reaffirmed America's commitment to a "strong, united, and democratic China" and dispatched Marshall to seek a truce and a coalition government between Chiang Kai-shek's Nationalists at Chungking and Mao Zedong's Communists in Yen-an. Neither side, however, had any intention of compromising with the other, and fighting resumed in October 1946. At first the United States imposed an arms embargo, but after May 1947 it extended aid to Chiang—a policy aptly described as "neutrality against the Communists."

Stalin, having blundered badly in China in the 1920s, kept up correct relations with the Nationalists on the assumption that Chiang was too strong to defeat but not strong enough to defy Soviet interests in Manchuria, Mongolia, and Sinkiang. The U.S.S.R. concluded a treaty of friendship with the Nationalist government on Aug. 14, 1945. Soviet policy at that time was to depict Mao as a mere agrarian reformer and to call for a coalition government. Having won Chiang's blessing, the Soviets systematically looted Manchuria of industrial equipment and reassumed their old rights on the Chinese Eastern railway. At the same time, Molotov insisted that the United States withdraw its advisers.

Chiang's forces advanced on all fronts until they captured Yen-an itself in March 1947, but the rapid occupation of North China and Manchuria, with American aid but against American advice, overextended the Nationalist army and tied it to cities and railroad lines. Corrupt officers also sold vast numbers of U.S. weapons to the enemy and siphoned off much of the $2,000,000,000 in U.S. aid into personal fortunes. When the Communists counterattacked at the end of 1947, Nationalist units were left isolated in the cities or simply melted away. The Communists took Tientsin and Peking in January 1949 and opened a southward offensive in April. By June their army had grown to 1,500,000 men and Chiang's had shrunk to 2,100,000. On August 5 a State Department White Paper announced the cessation of all aid to the Nationalists and concluded that "the ominous result of the civil war in China is beyond the control of the government of the United States." The remaining Nationalists fled to the island of Formosa (Taiwan), and the Communists officially proclaimed the People's Republic of China at Peking on Oct. 1, 1949. Only then did Stalin recognize the Maoist regime and negotiate to return Port Arthur and the Manchurian railway to Chinese control.

The fall of China to communism, following hard on the Berlin blockade and the first Soviet A-bomb test, was a terrific blow to the United States. The disaster gave Republicans a stick with which to beat the Truman administration, while the perjury of Alger Hiss (a high-ranking State Department officer, president of the Carnegie Endowment for World Peace, and erstwhile Communist agent) lent credence to charges that Communist sympathizers were at work in Washington. On Feb. 9, 1950, Senator Joseph R. McCarthy claimed to know the identities of 205 State Department officials tainted by Communism.

Nationalist soldiers retreat from an advancing Communist force near Pengpu, China, on December 17, 1948.

Over the course of four years of congressional hearings McCarthy used innuendo and intimidation to propound charges that, in virtually every case, proved groundless. Nonetheless, the tide of suspicion he incited—or exploited— ironically made him, as Truman said, "the greatest asset that the Kremlin has." Not only did his behaviour besmirch the image of the United States but it also bequeathed the charge of "McCarthyism" as an impregnable defense to be used by all manner of leftists.

The original question—"Who lost China?"—had been answered by the White Paper: America was not omnipotent and China was not America's to lose. Misperception of Asian realities and the "Europe-first" bias of the East Coast establishment, most Democrats, and the army certainly contributed to the debacle, however. "Asia-firsters," including the much less influential West Coast establishment, most Republicans, and the navy, rued the equanimity with which the administration witnessed the collapse of the Nationalists. For his part, Stalin must have found it equally mysterious that the United States would go to the brink of war over Berlin and spend billions to aid western Europe, then stand aside while the world's most populous nation went Communist and shrug that it would "wait for the dust to settle," as Secretary of State Dean Acheson put it.

The Korean War

Events in neighbouring Korea determined that the dust would not settle for another 20 years. In 1945 Soviet and American troops occupied the peninsula, ruled by Japan since 1910, on either side of the 38th parallel. In North Korea indigenous Marxists under Kim Il-sung took control with Soviet assistance and began to organize a totalitarian state. In South Korea General John R. Hodge, lacking firm instructions from Washington, began as early as the autumn of 1945 to establish defense forces and police and to move toward a separate administration. He also permitted the return of the nationalist leader Syngman Rhee. By the time Washington and Moscow noticed Korea, the Cold War had already set in and the de facto partition, as in Germany, became permanent. South and North Korean governments formally arose in 1948, each claiming legitimacy for the whole country and threatening to unify Korea by force. Between October 1949 and June 1950 several thousand soldiers were killed in border incidents along the parallel. The war that followed, therefore, was not so much a new departure as a denouement.

WAR BREAKS OUT

On Jan. 12, 1950, Acheson outlined his Asian policy in a speech before the Press Club in Washington, D.C. He included Japan, Okinawa, and the Philippines within the American line of defense but excluded Taiwan and Korea. Five months later, on June 25, 1950, the North Koreans invaded across the 38th parallel. Conventional wisdom had it that Kim was acting on Stalin's orders and that Acheson's omission had "invited" the attack. The declassification of documents of the period, however, has led to a reconsideration of the question of the origins of the Korean War. The United States had not ignored Korea;

On July 31, 1950, U.S. troops head toward the front lines of the Korean War.

rather, the State Department considered South Korea vital to the defense of Japan. It is more likely that Acheson's failure to mention Korea meant that the United States did not intend to station its own forces in Korea, unlike the countries mentioned, and that the United States was purposely withholding unequivocal support from Rhee lest he take it as encouragement to invade the north. Thus, Acheson was trying to prevent a war but probably trying also to ensure that if hostilities did occur the Communists would be to blame. Perhaps that is why he later referred to North Korea's attack not as an act of betrayal or aggression but as one of stupidity.

Stalin always behaved toward his client states with similar caution and strove to keep them under control. Why then should he "unleash" Kim and expose North Korea to a U.S. counterattack that might become a precedent for pushing communism back elsewhere? The possibility exists that Kim (like Ho Chi Minh) acted on his own in pursuit of a united national communist state. On the other hand, Stalin may indeed have encouraged North Korea to attack in order to keep Kim—and Mao—dependent on the U.S.S.R. or to create a costly diversion for the Americans. According to Khrushchev's memoirs, Kim initiated the idea of invading and Stalin, almost casually and certainly foolishly, approved it.

The Truman administration responded with alacrity, viewing Korea as a test case for the policy of containment. The United States appealed to the Security Council (which the Soviets were boycotting for its continued seating of Nationalist China) and obtained a condemnation of North Korea and an affirmation of collective security. Once the South Korean rout was evident, Truman ordered MacArthur to transfer forces from Japan to Korea, where they barely established a perimeter around the port of Pusan. Against Senator Robert A. Taft's protest of Truman's actions as a usurpation of Congress' right to declare war, most Americans accepted Truman's analogy with the 1930s and his determination not to appease the aggressor. Ultimately, 16 UN member states provided troops for this "police action," but U.S. and South Korean troops bore the brunt of the fighting.

In September 1950, following MacArthur's brilliant amphibious landing at Inch'ŏn, Truman approved operations north of the 38th parallel, and soon UN forces were driving through North Korea toward the Yalu River border with China. When the UN General Assembly adopted a U.S. resolution (October 7) to establish a unified, democratic Korea, it appeared that the Western alliance was going beyond containment to a "rollback" strategy: Communists who attacked others ran the risk of being attacked themselves. In November, however, contrary to MacArthur's confident predictions, Chinese forces attacked across the Yalu. By the new year, UN armies had retreated south of the 38th parallel and MacArthur demanded the right to expand the war. If American boys were dying, he asked, how could the government in good conscience fail to attack the enemy's home base or use every weapon at its disposal? Prime Minister Attlee, speaking for the allies, strongly opposed a wider war or the use of nuclear weapons. By April 1951 the UN forces had recaptured Seoul and regained the 38th parallel.

EFFECTS OF THE WAR

The effects of the Korean War reverberated around the world. Europeans feared that Korea was a diversion and that Stalin's real aim was to attack in Europe. Accordingly, Acheson agreed in September 1950 to contribute U.S. divisions to a NATO army under the command of General Eisenhower. "Asia-firsters" objected strenuously and kicked off what was known as "the great debate." Herbert Hoover even called for the United States to write off western Europe and to make the Western Hemisphere the "Gibraltar of Western Civilization." The Truman administration, backed by eastern Republicans and Eisenhower himself, persuaded Congress to commit four additional divisions to Europe. The Korean War also hastened implementation of NSC-68, a document drafted by Paul Nitze that called for a vigorous program of atomic and conventional rearmament to meet America's global commitments.

As American and allied publics grew increasingly impatient with the bloody deadlock in Korea, Truman determined to seek a negotiated peace. MacArthur tried to undermine this policy, issuing his own ultimatum to Peking and writing Congress that "there is no substitute for victory," whereupon in April 1951 Truman fired him for insubordination. The popular warrior and proconsul went home to a hero's welcome, and the Senate held hearings on the propriety of the "limited war" strategy. Marshall defended the president, arguing that a wider war in Asia would expose Europe to attack, while General Omar Bradley insisted that MacArthur's plans would "involve us in the wrong war, at the wrong place, at the wrong time and with the wrong enemy." MacArthur retorted that limited war was a form of appeasement.

Truce negotiations opened at Kaesŏng on July 10 after the Chinese had dropped their demands for withdrawal of all foreign troops from Korea and admission of the People's Republic to the UN in place of Nationalist China. The talks broke off in August, then resumed at P'anmunjŏm in October. Bitter fighting continued for two more years as each side sought to improve its tactical position. The talks centred on two issues: the demarcation line between North and South Korea and the repatriation of more than 150,000 Chinese and North Korean prisoners of war, many of whom did not want to return home. After hinting that the United States might resort to use of the atomic bomb, the newly elected president Dwight Eisenhower achieved an armistice signed at P'anmunjŏm on July 27, 1953, that separated the armies with a demilitarized zone along the 38th parallel and otherwise restored the *status quo ante bellum*. Chinese torture of U.S. prisoners and anti-American propaganda, combined with U.S. refusal to recognize the Peking regime and the conclusion of a defense treaty with Nationalist China (Taiwan), ensured continued hostility between Washington and Peking. Indeed, documents declassified in the late 1980s showed that both Truman and Eisenhower saw early on the potential for a Sino-Soviet split and that maximum pressure on Peking, not conciliation, was the way to bring it on.

Asian Wars and the Deterrence Strategy

While war raged in Korea, the French were battling the nationalist and Communist Viet Minh in Indochina. When a French army became surrounded at Dien Bien Phu in 1954, Paris appealed to the United States for air support. American leaders viewed the insurgency as part of the worldwide Communist campaign and at first propounded the theory that if Indochina went Communist other Southeast Asian countries would also fall "like dominoes." Eisenhower, however, was reluctant to send U.S. troops to Asian jungles, to appropriate war-making powers to the executive, or to sully the anti-imperialist reputation of the United States, which he considered an asset in the Cold War. In any case both he and the American people wanted "no more Koreas." Hence the United States supported partition of Indochina as the best means of containing the Viet Minh, and after French Premier Pierre Mendès-France came to power promising peace, partition was effected at the Geneva Conference of 1954. Laos and Cambodia won independence, while two Vietnams emerged on either side of the 17th parallel: a tough Communist regime under Ho Chi Minh in the north, an unstable republic in the south. National elections intended to reunite Vietnam under a single government were scheduled for 1956 but never took place, and, when the United States assumed France's former role as South Vietnam's sponsor, another potential "Korea" was created.

The Korean War and the new administration brought significant changes in U.S. strategy. Eisenhower believed that the Cold War would be a protracted struggle and that the greatest danger for the United States would be the temptation to spend itself to death. If the United States were obliged to respond to endless Communist-instigated "brushfire wars," it would soon lose the capacity and will to defend the free world. Hence Eisenhower and Secretary of State John Foster Dulles determined to solve "the great equation," balancing a healthy economy with only what was essential by way of military force. Their answer was a defense policy whereby the United States would deter future aggression with its airborne nuclear threat. As Dulles put it, the United States reserved the right to reply to aggression with "massive retaliatory power" at places of its own choosing.

In implementing this policy, Eisenhower cut overall defense spending by 30 percent over four years but beefed up the Strategic Air Command. The diplomatic side of this new policy was a series of regional pacts that linked the United States to countries ringing the entire Soviet bloc. Truman had already founded the NATO alliance, the ANZUS pact with Australia and New Zealand (1951), the Pact of Rio with Latin-American nations (1947), and the defense treaty with Japan (1951). Now Dulles completed an alliance system linking the 1954 Southeast Asia Treaty Organization (SEATO), stretching from Australia to Pakistan, to the 1955 Baghdad Pact Organization (later the

Central Treaty Organization [CENTO]), stretching from Pakistan to Turkey, to NATO, stretching from Turkey (after 1952) to Iceland.

Dulles viewed the postwar world in the same bipolar terms as had Truman and, for that matter, Stalin. Asian independence, however, not only expanded the arena of the Cold War but also spawned the third path of nonalignment. In April 1955 delegates from 29 nations attended the Bandung (Indonesia) Afro-Asian Conference, which was dominated by Nehru of India, Gamal Abdel Nasser of Egypt, and Sukarno of Indonesia. In theory the delegates met to celebrate neutrality and an end to "the old age of the white man"; in fact they castigated the imperialist West and praised, or tolerated, the U.S.S.R. Although most of the Bandung leaders were sloganeering despots in their own countries, the movement captivated the imagination of many guilt-ridden Western intellectuals.

The Suez Crisis

The Arab states, after their defeat in 1948, passed through a period of political unrest. The most critical change occurred in Egypt, where in 1952 a cabal of young army officers backed by the Muslim Brotherhood forced the dissolute King Farouk into exile. In 1954 Nasser emerged to assume control. Nasser envisioned a pan-Arab movement led by Egypt that would expel the British from the Middle East, efface Israel, and restore Islāmic grandeur. Egypt began sponsoring acts of violence against Israel from the Gaza Strip and cut off shipping through the Strait of Tīrān. The British were understandably hostile to Nasser, as were the French, who were battling Islāmic nationalists in Morocco, Algeria, and Tunisia.

Israel had used the years since 1948 to good effect, developing the arid country and training a reserve force of 200,000 men and women armed primarily with French weapons. Ben-Gurion believed that the Arabs would never accept the existence of Israel except by force. U.S. policy was to play down the Arab–Israeli dispute and alert all parties to the danger of Communist penetration. To this end, Eisenhower dispatched a futile mission in January 1956 in hopes of reconciling Cairo and Tel Aviv. In addition, the United States and Britain agreed to help finance Egypt's project for a new dam on the Nile at Aswān. Nasser's flirtations with Moscow, however, alienated Dulles, and the Americans and British both withdrew their support for the project. Then, on July 26, 1956, Nasser nationalized the Suez Canal, which had been owned by the French and British–influenced Suez Canal Company. He declared martial law in the canal zone and seized control of the Suez Canal Company, predicting that the tolls collected from ships passing through the canal would pay for the dam's construction within five years. Britain and France feared that Nasser might close the canal and cut off shipments of petroleum flowing from the Persian Gulf to western Europe.

The conservative Cabinet in London, the French, and the Israelis resolved to thwart Nasser. They could cite as precedent a CIA-backed coup d'état in Iran (August 1953) that overthrew the ascetic nationalist Mohammad Mosaddeq, who had expropriated foreign oil interests and also looked for support to the U.S.S.R. In any case, British, French, and Israeli planners met to work out a joint strike at the Sinai and Suez that might permit a far-reaching realignment in the Middle East. Eisenhower got wind of Israeli military preparations but believed that the blow would fall on Syria. He especially opposed hostilities before the U.S. election lest he lose Jewish votes by having to scold Israel. Moshe Dayan, the chief of staff of the Israeli armed forces, however, quietly mobilized all of Israel's mobile brigades, which struck on October 29 and took the Egyptians—and

the Americans—by surprise. Israeli war aims included the elim-
ination of the Egyptian army as an offensive threat,
neutralization of Palestinian bases in Gaza, and capture of the
Strait of Tīrān. The Anglo-French goals were to secure the Suez
Canal and possibly to topple Nasser and thus strike a blow at
Arab radicalism.

An Israeli airborne assault secured the Mitla Pass in the
Sinai while armoured columns penetrated the peninsula. The
Anglo-French then issued an ultimatum to Cairo and proceeded to bomb Egyptian bases. The Egyptian army evacuated
the Sinai. Eisenhower, preoccupied with the uprising in
Hungary and the U.S. election, was furious at this act of insubordination on the part of his allies and sponsored a UN
resolution for a cease-fire on November 1. Egypt frustrated the
Anglo-French plan by the simple expedient of scuttling ships

*In November 1956 Egyptian President Gamal Abdel Nasser ordered
the sinking of all ships at Port Said in order to block the British and
French from entering the Suez Canal.*

in the canal, but the Anglo-French went ahead with a landing at Port Said. The superpowers then forced an evacuation and the insertion of UN peacekeeping forces in the Sinai and Gaza Strip. There matters stood for 10 years.

Nasser emerged from the Suez Crisis a victor and a hero for the cause of Arab and Egyptian nationalism. Israel did not win freedom to use the canal, but it did regain shipping rights in the Straits of Tīrān. Britain and France, less fortunate, lost most of their influence in the Middle East as a result of the episode.

The only one who gained in the Suez muddle was the U.S.S.R. With the West in disarray and involved in a campaign that looked very much like old-fashioned imperialism, Soviet tanks returned to Budapest on November 4, crushed the Hungarians fighting with their homemade weapons, and liquidated their leaders. In 1957 the Soviets declared a new policy of "centralism" for the satellites and denounced both "dogmatism" (a code word for Stalinism) and "revisionism" (a code word for liberty).

The events of October 1956 nevertheless helped to renew momentum for European integration. The Hungarian uprising reminded western Europeans of the nature and proximity of the Soviet regime; Suez made them resentful of American tutelage. Inspired by Monnet and the Belgian economist Paul-Henri Spaak, "the Six" drafted the Euratom Treaty for a joint nuclear energy agency and the Treaty of Rome to expand the coal and steel community into a full-fledged Common Market. The treaties were signed on March 25, 1957, and went into effect on Jan. 1, 1958. The European Economic Community provided for internal and external tariff coordination, free movement of labour and capital, and a common agricultural pricing policy. Integration theorists hoped that international economic institutions would sustain a momentum leading to political unity as well.

Nuclear Weapons and the Balance of Terror

The postwar arms race began as early as 1943, when the Soviet Union began its atomic program and placed agents in the West to steal U.S. atomic secrets. When the U.S.S.R. rejected the Baruch Plan in 1946 and U.S.–Soviet relations deteriorated, a technological race became inevitable. The years of the U.S. monopoly, however, were a time of disillusionment for American leaders, who discovered that the atomic bomb was not the absolute weapon they had first envisioned. First, the atomic monopoly was something of a bluff. As late as 1948 the U.S. arsenal consisted of a mere handful of warheads and only 32 long-range bombers converted for their delivery.

Second, the military was at a loss as to how to use the bomb. Not until war plan "Half Moon" (May 1948) did the Joint Chiefs envision an air offensive "designed to exploit the destructive and psychological power of atomic weapons." Truman searched for an alternative, but balancing Soviet might in conventional forces with a buildup in kind would have meant turning the United States into a garrison state, an option far more expensive and damaging to civic values than nuclear weapons. A few critics, notably in the navy, asked how a democratic society could morally justify a strategy based on annihilation of civilian populations. The answer, which had been evolving since 1944, was that U.S. strategy aimed at deterring enemy attacks in the first place. "The only war you really win," said General Hoyt Vandenberg, "is the war that never starts."

Nuclear deterrence, however, was subject to at least three major problems. First, even a nuclear attack could not prevent the Soviet army from overrunning western Europe. Second, the nuclear threat was of no use in cases of civil war, insurgency, and other small-scale conflicts, a fact Stalin evidently relied on in several instances. Third, the U.S. monopoly was inevitably short-lived. By 1949 the Soviets had the atomic bomb, and the British joined the club in October 1952. The United States would be obliged to race indefinitely to maintain its technological superiority.

NEW TECHNOLOGY

The first contest in that race was for the "superbomb," a hydrogen, or fusion, bomb a thousand times more destructive than the atomic fission variety. Many scientists opposed this escalation. The dispute polarized the political and scientific communities. On the one hand it seemed as if the Cold War had created a climate of fear that no longer permitted principled dissent even on an issue involving human survival; on the other hand, it seemed as if the dissenters, inadvertently or not, were promoting the interests of the U.S.S.R. In January 1950, Truman gave his approval to the H-bomb project, and the first fusion bomb was tested successfully at Enewetak atoll in November 1952. No debate occurred in the Soviet Union, where scientists moved directly to fusion research and exploded their first bomb in August 1953.

In the meantime, Soviet agitprop agencies laboured abroad to weaken Western resolve. A prime target was NATO, which the Kremlin evidently viewed as a political threat (since its inferior order of battle was scarcely an offensive military threat). After 1950 the Soviets alternately wooed the western Europeans with assurances of goodwill and frightened them with assurances of their destruction if they continued to host American bases. Cominform parties and front organizations (such as the World Peace Council) denounced the Pentagon and U.S. "arms monopolies" and exploited fear and frustration to win

The first thermonuclear weapon (hydrogen bomb) was detonated at Enewetak atoll in the Marshall Islands, Nov. 1, 1952.

over intellectuals and idealists. The Stockholm Appeal of 1950, initiated by the French Communist physicist Frédéric Joliot-Curie, gathered petitions allegedly signed by 273,470,566 persons (including the entire adult population of the U.S.S.R.). Similar movements organized marches and protests in Western countries against nuclear arms (no such manifestations occurred in the Soviet bloc).

Eisenhower's defense policy brought a sharp increase in research and development of warheads and long-range bombers and the construction of air bases on the territory of allies circling the U.S.S.R. The H-bomb breakthrough, however, also triggered a race to develop intercontinental ballistic missiles (ICBMs). The United States entered the postwar era with an advantage in long-range rocketry, thanks to the suspension of the Soviet program during the war and the decision by the Germans' V-2 rocket team, led by Wernher von Braun, to surrender to the U.S. Army. In the budget-cutting of the late 1940s, however, the Truman administration surmised that the United States, possessed of superior air power and foreign bases, did not need long-range guided missiles. The first atomic weapons, bulky and of limited yield, also suggested that no rocket large and accurate enough to destroy a target 6,000 miles distant was then possible, but the vastly greater yield of fusion bombs and the expectation of smaller warheads changed that calculation. The U.S. ICBM project received top priority in June 1954. The Soviets, by contrast, needed to find a means of threatening the United States from Soviet soil. As early as 1947, therefore, Stalin gave priority to ICBM development.

ARMS CONTROL AND DEFENSE

How could the arms race be headed off before the world became locked into what Churchill called "the balance of terror"? The UN Disarmament Commission became a tedious platform for the posturings of the superpowers, the Americans insisting on on-site inspection, the Soviets demanding "general and complete disarmament" and the elimination of foreign bases. Eisenhower hoped that Stalin's death might help to break this deadlock. Churchill had been urging a summit conference ever since 1945, and once de-Stalinization and the Austrian State Treaty gave hints of Soviet flexibility, even Dulles acquiesced in a summit, which convened at Geneva in July 1955. The Soviets again called for a unified, neutral Germany, while the West insisted that it could come about only through

SPUTNIK

Although Soviet plans to orbit a satellite during the International Geophysical Year had been discussed extensively in technical circles, the October 4, 1957, launch of Sputnik 1 came as a surprise, and even a shock, to most people. Prior to the launch, skepticism had been widespread about the U.S.S.R.'s technical capabilities to develop both a sophisticated scientific satellite and a rocket powerful enough to put it into orbit.

Under Sergey Korolyov's direction, however, the Soviet Union had been building an intercontinental ballistic missile (ICBM), with engines designed by Valentin Glushko, that was capable of delivering a heavy nuclear warhead to American targets. That ICBM, called the R-7 or Semyorka ("Number 7"), was first successfully tested on August 21, 1957, which cleared the way for its use to launch a satellite. Fearing that development of the elaborate scientific satellite intended as the Soviet IGY contribution would keep the U.S.S.R. from being the first into space, Korolyov and his associates designed a much simpler 83.6-kg (184.3-pound) sphere carrying only two radio transmitters and four antennas. After the success of the R-7 in August, that satellite was rushed into production and became Sputnik 1. A second, larger satellite carrying scientific instruments and the dog Laika, the first living creature in orbit, was launched November 3. The even larger, instrumented spacecraft originally intended to be the first Soviet satellite went into orbit in May 1958 as Sputnik 3.

President Dwight D. Eisenhower, in May 1955, had committed the United States to an IGY satellite. The navy project, called Vanguard, would use a new launch vehicle based on modified Viking and Aerobee sounding rockets to orbit a small scientific satellite. Vanguard made slow progress over the subsequent two years, but, after Sputnik's success, the White House pressed to have the satellite launched as quickly as possible. On December 6, 1957, the Vanguard rocket rose only slightly off its launch pad before exploding and sending the satellite not into orbit but onto a Florida beach.

The Soviet Union was also the first to send a human into space. After a series of five test flights carrying dogs and human dummies, the first person, by that time designated as a cosmonaut, lifted into space in Vostok 1 atop a modified R-7 rocket on April 12, 1961, from the Soviet launch site at the Baikonur Cosmodrome in Kazakhstan. The passenger, Yury Gagarin, was a 27-year-old Russian test pilot.

free elections. On arms control, Eisenhower stunned the Soviets with his "open skies" proposal. The United States and the Soviet Union, he said, should exchange blueprints of all military installations and each allow the other side to conduct unhindered aerial reconnaissance. After some hesitation, Khrushchev denounced the plan as a capitalist espionage device. The Geneva summit marginally reduced tensions but led to no substantive agreements.

"Open skies" reflected the American fear of surprise attack. In 1954 a high-level "Surprise Attack Study" chaired by the scientist James Killian assured the President of a growing American superiority in nuclear weapons that would hold until the 1958–60 period but warned that the U.S.S.R. was ahead in long-range rocketry and would soon achieve its own secure nuclear deterrent. The panel recommended rapid development of ICBMs, construction of a distant early warning (DEW) radar line in the Canadian Arctic, strengthened air defenses, and measures to increase intelligence-gathering capabilities, both to verify arms control treaties and to avoid overreaction to Soviet advances. The Killian report gave birth to the U-2 spy plane, which began crisscrossing the U.S.S.R. above the range of Soviet air defense in 1956, and to a research program to develop reconnaissance satellites to observe the U.S.S.R. from outer space.

In 1955 both the United States and the Soviet Union announced programs to launch artificial Earth satellites during the upcoming International Geophysical Year (IGY). (The IGY was a worldwide program of geophysical research on the Earth and its planetary environment that was conducted from July 1957 to December 1958. The period was chosen to coincide with the maximum sunspot cycle.) The Eisenhower administration, concerned that the satellite program not interfere with military missile programs or prejudice the legality of spy satellites to come, entrusted its IGY proposal to the small, nonmilitary Vanguard rocket.

While Vanguard development crept ahead, the Soviet program won the first space race with Sputnik 1 on Oct. 4, 1957. The Soviet achievement shocked the Western world, challenged the strategic assumptions of every power, and thus inaugurated a new phase in the continuing Cold War.

CHAPTER 3

THE WORLD AFTER SPUTNIK

The concurrent arrival of the missile age and of an independent and restive Third World multiplied the senses in which politics had become global. Intercontinental rockets not only meant that the most destructive weapons known could now be propelled half-way around the world in minutes but also, because of the imminent nuclear standoff they heralded, that a Cold War competition would now extend into other realms—science and technology, economic growth, social welfare, race relations, image making—in which the Soviets or Americans could try to prove that their system was the best. At the same time, the decolonization of dozens of underdeveloped states in Asia and Africa induced the superpowers to look beyond the original front lines of the Cold War in Europe and East Asia.

These technological and political revolutions would seem to have raised the United States and the Soviet Union to unequaled heights of power. The Soviets and Americans advanced rapidly in the high technology required for space-flight and ballistic missiles, while techniques for the mobilization and management of intellectual and material resources reached a new level of sophistication, especially in the United States, through the application of systems analysis, computers, bureaucratic partnership with corporations and universities, and Keynesian "fine-tuning" of the economy.

By the mid-1960s the vigorous response of the Kennedy and Johnson administrations to the Cold War challenge seemed to ensure American technological, economic, and military primacy for the forseeable future. A mere five to seven years later, however, it became clear that the 1960s, far from establishing an American hegemony, had in fact wrought a diffusion of world power and an erosion of the formerly rigid Cold War blocs. Western Europe and Japan, now recovered from the war, also achieved dynamic economic growth in the 1960s, reducing their relative inferiority to the United States and prompting their governments to exercise a greater independence. The Sino-Soviet split, perhaps the most important event in postwar diplomacy, shattered the unity of the Communist bloc, and Third World countries often showed themselves resistant to superpower coercion or cajoling.

Soviet Progress and American Reaction

Premier Khrushchev anticipated the new correlation of forces in his foreign policy address to the 20th Party Congress in 1956. Soviet H-bombs and missiles, he said, had rendered the imperialists' nuclear threat ineffective, the U.S.S.R. an equal, the Socialist camp invincible, war no longer inevitable, and thus "peaceful coexistence" inescapable. In Leninist doctrine this last phrase implied a state of continued competition and Socialist advance without war. The immediate opportunities for Socialism, according to Khrushchev, derived from the struggle of the colonial peoples, which the U.S.S.R. would assist through foreign aid, propaganda, subversion, and support for "wars of national liberation."

The Soviet successes in outer space just 40 years after the Bolshevik Revolution were powerful evidence for Khrushchev's claims that the U.S.S.R. had achieved strategic equality and that Communism was the best system for overcoming backwardness. Sputnik restored Soviet prestige after the 1956 embarrassment in Hungary, shook European confidence in the U.S. nuclear deterrent, magnified the militancy of Maoist China, and provoked self-doubt in the United States itself. The two Sputnik satellites of 1957 were themselves of little military significance, and the test missile that launched them was too primitive for military deployment, but Khrushchev claimed that long-range missiles were rolling off the assembly line "like sausages," a bluff that allowed President Eisenhower's opponents—and nervous Europeans—to perceive a "missile gap." Khrushchev in turn tried to capitalize on the apparent gap in a series of crises, but his adventurous policy only provoked perverse reactions in China, the United States, and Europe that undermined his own political support at home.

Eisenhower was apprised in advance of Soviet missile progress thanks in part to overflights of the U-2 spy plane. By the time of Sputnik the Pentagon already had several parallel programs for ballistic missiles of various types, including the advanced, solid-fueled Polaris and Minuteman. The great fleet of B-47 and B-52 intercontinental bombers already deployed also assured continued American strategic superiority through the early 1960s. The frugal Eisenhower thus tried to play down the importance of Sputnik and to discourage a race for arms or prestige, but he was frustrated by a coalition of Democrats, journalists, academics, and hawks of both parties who insisted that the United States not only leapfrog the Soviets in space and missiles but also increase federal support to education, extend more military and economic aid to the Third World, and expand social programs at home intended in part to polish the American image abroad—in short, pursue the Cold War more vigorously.

Eisenhower conceded to this mood in 1958 by sponsoring creation of the National Aeronautics and Space Administration and passage of the National Defense Education Act, accelerating weapons programs, and deploying intermediate-range missiles in England, Italy, and Turkey. He also acknowledged the expanded Soviet threat in his State of the Union address in 1958: "Trade, economic development, military power, arts, science, education, the whole world of ideas—all are harnessed to this same chariot of expansion. The Soviets are, in short, waging total cold war." A similarly total American response to this challenge, requiring virtually wartime levels of national mobilization to outdo a totalitarian system in whatever field of endeavour it chose to emphasize, would, in Eisenhower's mind, however, have undermined the free market and fiscal soundness that were the foundation of American strength in the first place. Liberal economists argued in response that a sharply expanded role for the federal government was a matter of survival in the "space age" and would even stimulate economic growth, military prowess, and social progress.

The Sino-Soviet Split

A still more energetic U.S. retort would await the end of Eisenhower's term, but "Mr. Khrushchev's boomerang" (as Dulles termed Sputnik) had an immediate and disastrous impact on Soviet relations with the other Communist giant, China. Under their 1950 treaty of friendship, solidarity, and mutual assistance, Soviet technical aid flowed to Peking during the Korean War and helped support China's successful Five-Year Plan after 1953. Western observers looked in vain for ways to split the Communist bloc. As early as 1956, however, Chinese leaders showed displeasure over Khrushchev's denunciation of Stalin, the Kremlin's tendency to treat the Chinese party as it did those of the lesser satellites, and the new Soviet leaders themselves, whom Mao evidently considered mediocrities.

Mao also denounced "peaceful coexistence" as decadent and revisionist, a position shared by the tiny Stalinist dictatorship of Albania. Russian leadership in the world Communist movement was thus challenged for the first time.

Mao was a romantic revolutionary with an unquestionable bent for cruel or irrational theatrics on a gigantic scale. In the mid-1950s he paraded the slogan "Let a Hundred Flowers Bloom," ostensibly to encourage the voicing of new ideas on national development but perhaps rather to entice potential dissenters into revealing themselves. In 1958 this campaign was suddenly replaced by the "Great Leap Forward," by which all 700,000,000 Chinese were to form self-sufficient communes devoted to local industrialization. Large-scale industries and infrastructure collapsed, much to the disgust of Soviet guest engineers. By 1960–61 the economic chaos had become so severe that famine claimed 6,000,000–7,000,000 lives.

Nevertheless, the Chinese leadership seized upon Sputnik as proof that the "East wind" was prevailing over the "West wind" and insisted that the Soviets use their new superiority to press the revolution worldwide and, to the same end, provide China with atomic bombs and rockets. If the imperialists insisted on unleashing nuclear war, lectured Mao, and "half of mankind died, the other half would remain, while imperialism would be razed to the ground and the whole world become Socialist." The Soviets were appalled, especially since their superiority was, for the time being, a sham. At a November 1958 summit Mao learned that the Soviets would insist on retaining control over any warheads sent to China and would not share missile technology. When the Soviets also failed to back the Chinese in their 1958–59 conflicts with Taiwan and India, Sino-Soviet tensions increased. In the end Khrushchev refused to deliver a prototype nuclear warhead, whereupon the Chinese angrily repudiated "slavish dependence" on others and pledged to create their own nuclear arsenal. On July 16, 1960, the U.S.S.R. recalled all its specialists from China.

The Sino-Soviet split shattered the strict bipolarity of the Cold War world (though the United States would not take advantage of that fact for more than a decade) and turned the U.S.S.R. and China into bitter rivals for leadership in the Communist and Third worlds. The fundamental causes of the split must be traced to contradictions in the Soviet role as both the leader of the Communist movement and a great power with its own national interests. Before 1949 the U.S.S.R. had been able to subordinate the interests of foreign Communists to its own, but the Communist triumph in China, paradoxically, was a potential disaster for the U.S.S.R., for Mao and the Chinese would inevitably refuse to play the role of pupil. Once the Korean War was over and Stalin dead, the Chinese asserted themselves, learned the limits of "Socialist internationalism," and angrily began to plot their own course. While the ideological rift served, in the short run, to invigorate both Communist rivals as they competed for prestige and influence among the world's revolutionaries, it destroyed the myth that Communism transcended nationalism and power politics. This meant that the U.S.S.R. was delicately situated between the nuclear-armed NATO powers and the fanatical (and numerous) Chinese, and to appease either meant to alienate the other.

Accordingly, Khrushchev played a risky double game from 1958 to 1962, alternately holding out hope for arms control to the NATO powers and leveling demands backed by rocket-rattling. The historian Adam Ulam has seen in this a "grand design" by which Khrushchev hoped to ingratiate himself with the West (for instance, through a nuclear test-ban treaty) in return for the evacuation of West Berlin, recognition of the East German government, and permanent denial of nuclear weapons to West Germany—all of which might demonstrate

Soviet commitment to the Communist cause while providing a pretext for denial of nuclear weapons to China. Whether a grand design or an improvisation, Soviet diplomacy had to reckon at every turn with Peking's reactions and their likely effect on the rest of the Communist bloc.

Soviet Diplomatic Offensive

The Polish foreign minister, Adam Rapacki, was chosen to open Moscow's post-Sputnik campaign with a proposal to the UN General Assembly in October 1957 for a ban on nuclear weapons in Poland, Czechoslovakia, and the two Germanies. This initiative, like others before and after, was a no-lose strategem for the U.S.S.R. Given the Warsaw Pact's superiority in conventional weapons, any reduction of the West's nuclear deterrent in Europe stood to weaken NATO, even as the burden of seeming to oppose arms control would fall on the West if it refused. At the same time, the U.S.S.R. combined open and covert support for Western antinuclear movements with loud reminders of its ability to destroy any nation that foolishly hosted American bases.

NATO leaders resisted the Rapacki Plan but had immediately to deal with a March 1958 Soviet offer to suspend all nuclear testing provided the West did the same. Throughout the 1950s growing data on the harmful effects of nuclear fallout had been increasing pressure on the nuclear powers to take such a step. The United States and Britain were caught in the midst of testing warheads for the many new missiles under development, but a one-year test ban did go into effect in November 1958. With the Chinese making noises about a Soviet sellout to the West, however, Khrushchev immediately provoked a new crisis in Berlin, demanding that the Allies withdraw from West Berlin within six months. Khrushchev also indicated that the best way to solve the Berlin question would be to neutralize and disarm the two German states. In January 1959 the Soviets expanded their proposed nuclear-free zone to include East Asia and the whole Pacific Ocean area—a clear hint of their desire to prevent China from going nuclear.

The Berlin deadline passed without incident as Khrushchev accepted an invitation to become the first Soviet premier to visit the United States. Increasingly, the United States and the U.S.S.R. came to the same realization: each had interests in coexistence that outweighed their ideological loyalties. This was made manifest in August 1958, when Chinese artillery began an intense bombardment of the Nationalist-held off-shore islets of Quemoy and Matsu. Peking may have hoped to force Moscow to support its claim to sovereignty over Taiwan, while Chiang may have hoped to drag the United States into

Nikita Khrushchev (wearing medals) talks with President Dwight D. Eisenhower (holding ball) and Vice President Richard Nixon (next to Eisenhower) during the Soviet premier's visit to United States in September 1959.

supporting an invasion of the mainland. Neither superpower, however, was willing to risk war. The U.S. 7th Fleet resupplied Chiang's forces, while the Soviets pledged to defend mainland China, but both discouraged offensive action.

By September 1959, when Khrushchev arrived in the United States, Dulles had died, and Eisenhower was intent to use personal diplomacy in an attempt to put a cap on the arms race. The tour itself—from New York City to Iowa to Hollywood— was a sensation, though Khrushchev professed distaste for American consumerism and predicted "your grandchildren will live under Communism." His talks with Eisenhower produced an ephemeral "spirit of Camp David" and the scheduling of a follow-up summit conference for May 1960 in Paris.

Meanwhile, Khrushchev's last-ditch efforts to mend relations with Peking exploded in the spring of 1960. Mao himself reportedly authored an article cryptically condemning Khrushchev's détente policy as vile revisionism and reiterating Chinese willingness to confront nuclear war. The Chinese observer at a Warsaw Pact meeting in February 1960 declared in advance that any arms agreements reached at the U.S.– Soviet summit would not be binding on Peking. On the eve of the Paris summit an American U-2 spy plane was shot down over the U.S.S.R. When Eisenhower refused to apologize for the incident and assumed personal responsibility, Khrushchev had little choice but to walk out.

Decolonization and Development

Events in the other new arena of the post-Sputnik era—the Third World—likewise antagonized relations among the U.S.S.R., the United States, and China. All three assumed that the new nations would naturally opt for the democratic institutions of their mother countries or, on the other hand, would gravitate toward the "anti-imperialist" Soviet or Maoist camps. The United States had urged Britain and France to dismantle their empires in the aftermath of World War II, but, once those countries became Washington's most potent allies in the Cold War, the United States offered grudging support for Anglo-French resistance to nationalist and Communist forces in their colonies.

President Truman's Point Four Program mandated U.S. foreign aid and loans to new nations lest they "drift toward poverty, despair, fear, and the other miseries of mankind which breed unending wars." When the Eisenhower administration cut back on foreign aid, a great debate about its efficacy ensued among American experts. Critics insisted that the Marshall Plan was not a valid analogy for Third World aid because the former had been a case of helping industrial populations rebuild their societies, while the latter was a case of sparking industrial or even merely agricultural development in primitive economies. Foreign aid did not necessarily serve U.S. interests, since many Third World rulers chose neutralism or Socialism, nor did it promote economic growth, since most new nations lacked the necessary social and physical infrastructure for a modern economy. Proponents of aid replied that U.S. capital and technology were needed precisely to build infrastructure, to assist "nation building," and to fortify recipients against Communists and others who might subvert the development process in its early stages. In the late 1950s, U.S. economic aid averaged about $1,600,000,000 per year, compared with about $2,100,000,000 in military aid to friendly regimes.

The Soviet line, by contrast, held that new nations would not be truly independent until they freed themselves from economic dependence on their former masters, but the Soviets invariably expected a political return for their own assistance. The claim of the People's Republic of China to be the natural leader of Third World revolt also obliged Khrushchev to make bolder endorsements of wars of national liberation. By 1960 it was already clear, however, that local politics and culture made every Third World situation unique.

The Middle East had reached an unstable deadlock based precariously on the UN-administered cease-fire of 1956. The eclipse of British and French influence after the Suez debacle made the United States fearful of growing Soviet influence in the region, symbolized by the Soviet offer to take over construction of the Aswān High Dam in Egypt. In January 1957 the U.S. Congress authorized the president to deploy U.S. troops in the region if necessary and to dispense $500,000,000 in aid to friendly states. This Eisenhower Doctrine appeared to polarize the region, with Middle East Treaty Organization members in support and Egypt, Syria, and Yemen in opposition. When, in July 1958, nationalist generals backed by a variety of factions, prominent among which were Communists, overthrew the pro-Western Hāshimite monarchy in Iraq, and unrest spread to Jordan and Lebanon, Eisenhower responded at once. The 14,000 U.S. troops that landed in Beirut allowed the Lebanese president to restore order on the basis of a delicate compromise among radical, Muslim, and Christian factions. Khrushchev denounced the intervention, demanded that the U.S.S.R. be consulted, and tried without success to convene an international conference on the Middle East. His extension of an invitation to India, but not China, needlessly alienated Peking and signaled a new Soviet interest in relations with New Delhi.

The climactic year of African decolonization was 1960, and the first Cold War crisis on that continent occurred when, in that year, Belgium hastily pulled out of the vast Belgian Congo (now Congo [Kinshasa]). Tribal antagonisms and rival personalities made even the independence ceremonies a catastrophe, as the Congolese nationalist leader and first prime minister, Patrice Lumumba, supported an insurrection by Congolese army units that involved the murder of whites and blacks alike. No sooner had Belgian troops returned to restore order than Moise Tshombe declared the secession of the iron-rich Katanga province. UN Secretary-General Dag Hammarskjöld intervened against the Belgians and Katangese (thereby setting an ominous precedent of UN toleration for black violence against blacks or other races), while the Soviets accused Tshombe of being a dupe for imperialist mining interests and threatened to send arms and Soviet "volunteers" to the leftist Lumumba. Hammarskjöld then organized a UN armed force to subdue Katanga and save the Congo—and Africa—from Cold War involvement.

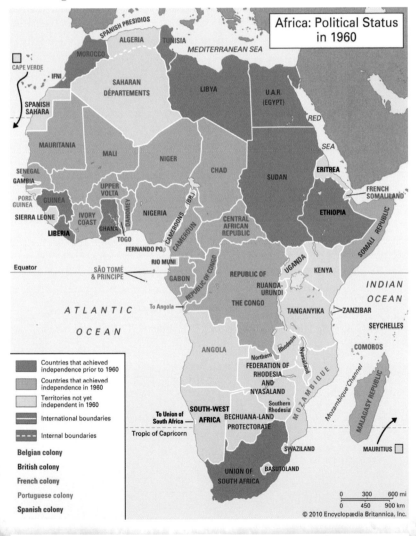

Africa: Political Status in 1960

Countries that achieved independence prior to 1960
Countries that achieved independence in 1960
Territories not yet independent in 1960
International boundaries
Internal boundaries

Belgian colony
British colony
French colony
Portuguese colony
Spanish colony

0   300   600 mi
0   450   900 km
© 2010 Encyclopædia Britannica, Inc.

The political status of African states in 1960.

The clumsy UN efforts did not prevent, and may have incited, the spread of civil war. Lumumba tried to establish his own secessionist state, but he then fell into the hands of the Congolese army headed by Joseph Mobutu (later Mobutu Sese Seko), a former sergeant, and was murdered by the Katangese in January 1961. Hammarskjöld himself died in a plane crash in the Congo in September 1961. UN troops remained until 1964, but as soon as they were withdrawn rebellion returned, and Mobutu seized control in a military coup d'état in 1965. The Katangan revolt was not quelled until 1967.

In Southeast Asia the Geneva Accords disintegrated rapidly after 1954. The planned elections to reunify Vietnam were never held, since South Vietnam's leader, Ngo Dinh Diem, both feared the results and denied the possibility of free elections in the Communist north. Ho Chi Minh's regime in Hanoi then trained 100,000 native southerners for guerrilla war and launched a campaign of assassination and kidnapping of South Vietnamese officials. In December 1960 the Viet Cong (as Diem dubbed them) proclaimed the formation of a National Liberation Front (NLF), with the avowed aim of reuniting the two Vietnams under a Hanoi regime. American advisers tried vainly to arrest the disintegration of South Vietnam with advice on counterinsurgency and state-building techniques.

In neighbouring Laos the Communist Pathet Lao took control of the two northernmost provinces of the country in defiance of the neutral government under Prince Souvanna Phouma agreed upon after Geneva. Those provinces sheltered the Ho Chi Minh Trail supply route bypassing the demilitarized zone between the two Vietnams. When a new, assertive Laotian government sent troops to enforce its authority over the provinces in 1958–59, civil war appeared inevitable. A military coup d'état led by Kong Le briefly returned Souvanna to power, but when Kong Le was in turn driven out in December

1960, he joined forces with the Pathet Lao in their strategic stronghold in the Plain of Jarres. Having secured the Laotian territory needed for infiltration and assault on South Vietnam, North Vietnam persuaded China and the U.S.S.R. in December 1960 to approve Ho's plan for a "nonpeaceful transition to socialism" in Vietnam.

Latin-American Problems

Finally, Cold War rivalry and Third World problems intersected devastatingly in America's own backyard. Before the era of Roosevelt's Good Neighbor Policy, the United States had frequently been accused of meddling too much in the affairs of other states in the hemisphere. By the 1950s the contradictory charge was leveled that the United States was not involving itself enough, as evidenced by the fact that the United States spent $12,600,000,000 on aid to Asia and the Middle East in the period 1953–57 compared with $1,900,000,000 on Latin America. Resentment over the CIA's role in toppling an allegedly Communist-backed government in Guatemala in 1954 and violent protests against Vice President Richard M. Nixon during his trip to Caracas and Lima in 1958 alerted Washington to the dangers inherent in neglecting the genuine needs of the region. The United States agreed to fund an Inter-American Development Bank, while the State Department sought to avoid too close an association with unpopular, authoritarian regimes. Whatever the overall merits of such a policy, it had immediate and disastrous effects in Cuba.

In 1952 Fulgencio Batista established a corrupt dictatorship in Cuba, and four years later a young revolutionary named Fidel Castro took to the Sierra Maestra with 150 comrades and made pretensions of fighting a guerrilla war. In fact, Castro's campaign was largely propaganda (the insurgents lost only 40

THE CUBAN REVOLUTION

For much of the 1950s, the corrupt Cuban dictator Fulgencio Batista exercised absolute control over the political system. By the end of the decade, Cuba had developed one of the leading economies in Latin America, with an annual income of $353 per capita in 1958—among the highest in the region. Yet economic disparities grew, and most rural workers earned only about one-fourth the average per year. Although the thriving economy enriched a few Cubans, the majority experienced poverty (especially in the countryside), an appalling lack of public services, and unemployment and underemployment. U.S. and other foreign investors controlled the economy, owning about 75 percent of the arable land, 90 percent of the essential services, and 40 percent of the sugar production.

Batista's fall resulted as much from this internal decay as from the challenges of revolutionary groups. Fidel Castro, who had been a legislative candidate for elections in 1952 that were aborted by Batista, led the 26th of July movement, named after his failed attack on the Moncada military base in Santiago on July 26, 1953. His defense of his part in the attack, edited and published as "History Will Absolve Me," was a political manifesto. Released from prison in 1955, Castro and some friends went to Mexico to prepare for the overthrow of the Cuban government. In December 1956 the small yacht *Granma* landed Castro and a band of rebels in southeastern Cuba, where they were routed and almost annihilated by security forces. A dozen survivors, including Castro, his brother Raúl, and the Argentine revolutionary Che Guevara, retreated to the Sierra Maestra and began a guerrilla campaign. Over the next two years they attracted hundreds of Cuban volunteers, won several battles over Batista's increasingly demoralized armed forces, and advanced westward across the island. Meanwhile, communist groups and radical members of the Federation of University Students, a noncommunist organization, staged strikes and attacks in urban areas. In 1958 the United States isolated Batista's government with an arms embargo, and several Cuban military commanders sympathized with the rebellion or joined it. Batista fled the country on the morning of January 1, 1959, and on his heels about 800 of Castro's supporters marched into Havana, having defeated an army of some 30,000.

The 26th of July Movement had vague political plans, relatively insignificant support, and totally untested governing skills. They quickly forged a following among poor peasants, urban workers, youths, and idealists. The Communist Party of Cuba, dating to 1925, assumed the dominant political role, and the state modeled itself on the Soviet-bloc countries of eastern Europe, becoming the first socialist country in the Americas.

The regime progressively dissolved the capitalist system in Cuba by establishing a centrally planned economy, collectivizing agricultural production (except for a small percentage of farmland), forming close economic ties with the Soviet Union, and developing a range of social services, particularly in rural areas. It also eliminated the remnants of Batista's army and created new institutions to replace the former labour unions, political parties, and associations of professional workers and farmers. The regime nationalized hundreds of millions of dollars in U.S. property and private businesses, which provoked retaliatory measures by the U.S. government, including a trade embargo, an unsuccessful invasion by Cuban exiles at the Bay of Pigs in south-central Cuba (April 1961), and unexecuted plots to assassinate Castro. However, the U.S. stance only solidified Castro's popular support and further pushed him toward the Soviet Union. In December he declared himself a communist.

men in the largest engagement), and the real struggle for Cuba was fought out in the arenas of Cuban and American public opinion. After Nixon's tour, liberal opinion and the State Department deserted Batista, and the new ambassador to Havana was ordered to preside over his fall. In March 1958 the

United States suspended arms sales to Cuba, and on Jan. 1, 1959, a triumphant Castro entered Havana without the necessity of fighting a battle. Contrary to his image as a populist and democrat, Castro made himself the new dictator, nationalized hundreds of millions of dollars worth of American property, and declared that he was and always had been a Marxist. His actions gradually alienated whatever sympathy he had in the United States. Castro invited Soviet aid and came to rely on it heavily after the United States curtailed Cuba's sugar import quota in July 1960. Eisenhower instructed the CIA to explore means of removing Castro, who made Cuba into an immensely valuable Soviet satellite 90 miles from the United States.

By 1960, therefore, the post-Sputnik world posed new challenges for the Western alliance stretching from outer space to Third World jungles. Polls showed that a majority of western Europeans believed Khrushchev's propaganda about Soviet superiority and that a majority of Americans no longer believed in Eisenhower's low-key approach to Cold War issues.

Policies of the Kennedy Administration

The inauguration of John F. Kennedy as president of the United States infused American foreign policy with new style and vigour. He had promised to "get America moving again," and he appointed a Cabinet and staff who shared his belief that the United States could be doing far more to prove its technological and moral superiority over the U.S.S.R., win the "hearts and minds" of Third World peoples, and accelerate social progress at home. His administration also overturned Eisenhower's policy on economy and defense and held that Keynesian fiscal policy and large programs for research, education, and human resources would foster the rapid growth needed to pay for the new federal activism.

Kennedy's inaugural address was thus an exhortation and warning: "Let every nation know, whether it wishes us well or ill, that we shall pay any price, bear any burden, meet any hardship, support any friend, oppose any foe to assure the survival and the success of liberty." He and Secretary of Defense Robert McNamara accordingly increased the U.S. defense budget by 30 percent in their first year in office and approved deployment of a strategic triad of weapons—the land-based Minuteman ICBMs, submarine-launched Polaris missiles, and B-52 bombers. The Kennedy advisers had also been highly critical of the policy of reliance on massive retaliation and determined to make the United States capable of flexible response by expanding conventional armed forces as well. Kennedy paid special attention to the training of counterinsurgency "special forces."

THIRD WORLD FOREIGN AID

On May 25, 1961, Kennedy told a joint session of Congress that "the great battlefield for the defense and expansion of freedom today is the whole southern half of the globe—Asia, Latin America, Africa, and the Middle East." The enemies of freedom were seeking to capture these rising peoples "in a battle of minds and souls as well as lives and territories." Expanded aid programs, the Peace Corps, active promotion of democracy through the U.S. Information Agency, and military support against guerrilla warfare would, he declared, all help in cases "where the local population is too caught up in its own misery to be concerned about the advance of Communism." Kennedy also underscored the impact of the Soviet space program on world opinion (Yuri Gagarin had become the first man to orbit the Earth on April 12) and asked that Congress commit the United States to a program to land a man on the Moon by 1970. Kennedy's call for the creation of an International Telecommunications Satellite Consortium bespoke his desire to associate the United States with the peaceful uses of outer space.

The new attitude toward the Third World was perhaps the clearest break in American diplomacy. Basing its policy on W.W. Rostow's "non-Communist manifesto" describing stages of economic development, the Kennedy administration increased foreign aid for Third World nations whether or not they were politically aligned with the United States. The Alliance for Progress, created in March 1961, especially targeted Latin America. By 1965 U.S. foreign aid reached $4,100,000,000 as compared with $2,300,000,000 contributed by all other developed countries. The validity of Rostow's investment model for economic "takeoff" was debated for two decades, but perhaps the greatest weakness in U.S. aid programs was the assumption that local rulers could be persuaded to put their own people's welfare first. Instead, aid money often fed corruption, bolstered power-hungry leaders or Socialist bureaucracies, or helped to finance local conflicts. What was more, the Soviets had some natural advantages in dealing with such leaders, since they offered no moralistic advice about democracy and human rights, while their own police-state methods served the needs of local despots.

On the other hand, sustained world economic growth and measures to stabilize commodity prices helped the developing countries to achieve an average annual growth rate of 5 percent during the 1960s (compared with 5.1 percent for industrial countries). But the crushing rate of Third World population growth (2.6 percent annually) meant that even in the best of times foreign aid only just offset the effects of Third World fertility.

THE BAY OF PIGS AND THE BERLIN WALL

Kennedy's first crisis stemmed from his endorsement of the CIA plan to unseat Castro. The CIA had trained Cuban exiles in Guatemala and flown them to Florida, whence they were to stage an invasion of Cuba in expectation of a popular revolt there. Instead, the landing at the Bay of Pigs on April 17, 1961, was a fiasco. No coordination had been achieved with dissidents inside Cuba, while the failure to provide U.S. air cover (perhaps for fear of retaliation in Berlin) doomed the invasion. Castro's army killed or captured most of the 1,500-man force in two days. The U.S.S.R. reaped a propaganda harvest and pledged to defend Cuba in the future. Kennedy had to content himself with a promise to resist any efforts by Castro and the guerrilla leader Che Guevara to export revolution elsewhere in Latin America.

Members of Assault Brigade 2506, as the CIA-trained Cuban exiles were known, were captured in the Bay of Pigs on April 17, 1961.

Kennedy and Khrushchev held a summit meeting in Vienna in June 1961. With Berlin and the Third World uppermost in his mind, Kennedy proposed that neither superpower attempt to upset the existing balance of power in any region where the other was already involved. Khrushchev evidently considered the young president to be weak and on the defensive and tried to intimidate him with a new ultimatum, threatening to turn over control of Western access to West Berlin to the East German government. (Khrushchev was being pressured by the East German leader Walter Ulbricht to stem the tide of thousands of skilled workers who were fleeing across the zonal boundary into West Berlin.) Kennedy responded by pledging to defend West Berlin and calling up 250,000 reservists.

On Aug. 13, 1961, Soviet and East German troops closed down interallied checkpoints and proceeded to build the Berlin Wall, sealing off the western city. Just as in 1948, the U.S. leadership debated whether to respond with force to this violation of the Potsdam Accords, but the hesitancy of the NATO allies and the timidity—or prudence—of Kennedy limited the West to a reassertion of access rights to West Berlin. Kennedy then made a dramatic visit to West Berlin, where he told a cheering crowd, "Today, in the world of freedom, the proudest boast is 'Ich bin ein [I am a] Berliner.' "

The Cuban Missile Crisis

In the midst of this crisis the Soviets unilaterally broke the moratorium on nuclear testing, staging a series of explosions yielding up to 50 megatons. Soviet technology had also perfected a smaller warhead for the new Soviet missiles now ready to be deployed, like the Minuteman, in hardened silos. Khrushchev, his nation still behind in strategic nuclear firepower, tried to redress the balance by insinuating 42 medium-range missiles into Cuba, whence they could reach most of the continental United States. He apparently hoped that these missiles, once in place, could then serve as a bargaining chip in negotiations leading to a neutralized Germany, which in turn might help Moscow persuade the Chinese to cease their own nuclear program. Instead, the ploy brought the world to the brink of war. On Oct. 14, 1962, U-2 spy planes photographed the missile sites under construction in Cuba. Two days later Kennedy convened a secret crisis-management committee that leaned at first toward a surgical air strike to destroy the sites. The president, however, opted for a less risky response: a naval quarantine to prevent Soviet freighters from reaching Cuba and an ultimatum demanding that the bases be dismantled and the missiles removed.

On October 18, Soviet Ambassador Andrey Gromyko met with Kennedy and denied that the U.S.S.R. had any offensive intentions with respect to Cuba. On October 22 the President informed the nation of the crisis and called on Khrushchev to pull back from "this clandestine, reckless, and provocative threat to world peace." For two days the world waited anxiously, and on the 24th Soviet ships in transit abruptly changed course away from Cuba. On the 26th Khrushchev sent Kennedy a message offering to withdraw the missiles in exchange for a U.S. pledge never to invade Cuba. The next day a harsher message arrived with a new demand that the United States withdraw its own missiles from Turkey. Those antiquated Jupiters, deployed in the early post-Sputnik scare, were already due for removal, but Kennedy would not do so under Soviet threat. Hence Attorney General Robert Kennedy suggested a ploy: simply reply to Khrushchev's first note as if the second had never been sent. On the 28th the Soviets agreed to dismantle the Cuban bases in return for a no-invasion pledge. Several months later the United States quietly removed its missiles from Turkey.

The Cuban missile crisis seemed at the time a clear victory for Kennedy and the United States and was widely attributed to American superiority in nuclear weapons. In fact, neither side showed the slightest willingness even to bluff a nuclear strike, and it was probably the overwhelming U.S. superiority in conventional naval and air power in its home waters that left the U.S.S.R. no option but retreat.

Nor was the crisis an unmitigated American victory. Kennedy's pledge never to overthrow Castro by force meant that the United States would have to tolerate whatever mischief he, backed by $300,000,000 a year in Soviet aid, might contrive in the future. To be sure, Kennedy warned that the United States would never tolerate any expansion of Communism in the hemisphere. (This pledge was underwritten by Lyndon Johnson in 1965 when he sent U.S. troops into the Dominican Republic to prevent a leftist takeover, but such interventionism only reminded Latin Americans of past "Yankee imperialism" and gave credence to Castro's anti-American propaganda.) The existence of a Communist base in the Caribbean, therefore, was to be a source of unending vexation for future American presidents. What is more, the Cuban missile crisis hardened Soviet determination never again to be humiliated by military inferiority. Khrushchev and his successors accordingly began the largest peacetime military buildup in history, which, by the 1970s, accorded the Soviet Union parity with the United States in nuclear forces and the ability to project naval power into every ocean of the world.

On the other hand, the Cuban missile crisis marked the final frustration of Khrushchev's efforts to force a German peace treaty and prevent the deployment of nuclear weapons on German or Chinese soil. Peking, of course, had supported the Soviets' bid to place missiles in Cuba and had taken the opportunity to attack India, and the precipitous Soviet retreat prompted Chinese charges of "capitulationism." The Chinese nuclear program proceeded apace, with the People's Republic exploding its first atomic device in 1964. Never again would the Soviet leadership hope to control the foreign policy of the other Communist giant.

Renewed U.S.–Soviet Cooperation

U.S.–Soviet relations, by contrast, markedly improved after the sobering visit to the brink of war. Hopes for a comprehensive nuclear test-ban treaty ran afoul of the U.S.S.R.'s customary refusal to permit on-site inspection to monitor underground tests, but a partial Test-Ban Treaty was signed by the United States, Britain, and the U.S.S.R. on Aug. 5, 1963, prohibiting nuclear explosions in the air, under the sea, and in outer space. The superpowers also established a direct communications link between Washington and Moscow for use in crisis situations. Other powers anxious to join the nuclear club, notably China and France, refused to adhere to the Test-Ban Treaty. Instead, the Chinese denounced Soviet collaboration with "the leader of world imperialism." Mao resurrected all of China's territorial claims against the Soviet Union dating from tsarist Russian imperialism and advocated partition of the Soviet empire. The Soviets, in turn, branded Mao with their most hateful current epithet: he was "another Stalin."

President Kennedy was assassinated on Nov. 22, 1963, and Khrushchev was removed from power by the Politburo in October 1964, a victim of his own failures in foreign policy and agriculture and of the Communist Party's resistance to his attempted reforms. The bilateral effort to pursue arms control survived under President Johnson and under Leonid Brezhnev and Aleksey Kosygin. The Outer Space Treaty ratified in 1967 banned nuclear weapons and other weapons of mass destruction in the Earth's orbit and on the Moon. A U.S.–Soviet draft Non-proliferation Treaty was also adopted by the UN in June 1968. (Once again, France, China, India, Pakistan, and Israel refused to sign.)

None of the arms-control instruments of the 1960s, however, put a cap on the arms race or restrained the signatories from doing anything in the strategic area they had a desire to do anyway. The superpowers were able to modernize their arsenals through underground nuclear testing; outer space was an awkward and vulnerable place to deploy warheads in any case; and neither superpower had an interest in seeing nuclear weapons spread to more countries. Rather, American nuclear policy aimed, at least in the short run, at ensuring the continued stability of U.S.–Soviet deterrence, lately dubbed "mutual assured destruction." Adopting the views of the strategist Bernard Brodie, McNamara concluded early on that the Soviets must eventually catch up and that a state of parity was the best that could be achieved in the nuclear age. Soon each side would be capable of obliterating the other in a retaliatory strike, even after a sneak attack. At that point, any attempt by either side to achieve an illusory superiority would only destabilize the balance and tempt one or the other into launching a first strike. Whether the Soviets ever shared this doctrine of deterrence is dubious. Marshal Sokolovsky's volumes on military strategy in the 1960s, while granting that nuclear war would be an unprecedented disaster for all, still committed the U.S.S.R. to a war-winning capability.

China, meanwhile, succumbed to another series of Maoist actions that completed that country's drift into chaos and isolation. In February 1966, Mao gave the nod to the young and fanatical Red Guards to make, by force, a Cultural Revolution.

Violence swallowed up schools, factories, bureaucracies, cultural institutions, and everything that smacked of foreign or traditional Chinese influence. Countless victims suffered internal exile, public humiliation, forced "self-criticism," or death, while attacks on foreign embassies and denunciations of the superpower "condominium" persuaded Americans and Soviets alike that the Chinese were, for the moment at least, the major threat to world peace.

By the late 1960s, therefore, relations between the United States and the Soviet Union underwent a marked thawing. At the same time, however, the Soviets and Americans alike had to acknowledge a growing lack of control over their once coherent Cold War camps.

Divergent Paths for Britain and France

The Suez crisis of 1956, followed by Soviet space successes and rocket-rattling after 1957, dealt serious blows to the morale of western Europe. Given the potential of the war scares over Berlin to fracture NATO, the United States had to reassure its allies and try to satisfy their demands for greater influence in alliance policy. American efforts largely succeeded in the case of Britain, an ally much depleted in power and will. American policy largely failed in the case of France, an ally stronger and more stable than at any time since 1940.

THE BRITISH EMPIRE COLLAPSES

Since World War II, Britain had tried to maintain the appearance of a global power, developing its own nuclear weapons, deploying conventional forces around the world, and keeping hold of its African colonies. Churchill, returned to office in the early 1950s, had vowed never to "preside over the liquidation of the British Empire." Likewise, the British held aloof from the continental experiments with integration and saw their role rather as the vertex of three great world systems: the English-speaking peoples, the British Commonwealth, and the old European Great Powers. All this came to a sudden end when a combination of factors—sluggish economic performance by the world's oldest industrial power, growing pressure to decolonize, demands for greater social expenditures at home, and the superpowers' leap into the missile age—convinced London that it could no longer afford to keep up appearances in foreign policy.

A defense White Paper of 1957 signalled a shift away from conventional armed forces toward reliance on a cheap, national nuclear deterrent. Sputnik then convinced the British government to cancel its own ballistic-missile program and rely on its special relationship with the United States to procure modern weapons. Eisenhower agreed to sell the Skybolt air-launched missile to Britain by way of healing the wounds inflicted by Suez and shoring up NATO after Sputnik. When McNamara subsequently cut the Skybolt program in his campaign to streamline the Pentagon, the British government was acutely embarrassed. Kennedy met with Prime Minister Harold Macmillan at Nassau in December 1962 and offered Polaris submarines instead. It was hoped at the time that the British deterrent would be subsumed in a multilateral NATO force. The Conservative government also made the hard decision in 1963 to seek admission to the Common Market, only to be vetoed by the French. Not until 1973 was Britain's application, together with those of Ireland and Denmark, approved and the European Communities broadened.

The period 1957–62 was also the climax of Britain's decolonization. As early as 1946–47, when Britain was granting independence to India and states of the Middle East, the Attlee government sponsored the Cohen–Caine plan for a new approach to West Africa as well. It aimed at preparing tropical Africa for self-rule by gradually transferring local authority from tribal chiefs to members of the Western-educated elite. Accordingly, the Colonial Office drafted elaborate constitutions, most of which had little relevance to real conditions in primitive countries that had no natural boundaries, no ethnic unity or sense of nationalism, and no civic tradition. When the Gold Coast (Ghana) elected the radical leader Kwame Nkrumah, who then demanded imme-diate independence and got it in 1957, the British felt unable to deny similar grants to neighbouring colonies. Britain had, in fact, when the matter was faced squarely, little desire to hang on, given the exorbitant financial and political costs of late imperialism.

In 1959 the Cabinet quietly decided to withdraw from Africa as soon as it won reelection. Macmillan then announced the new policy in Cape Town on Feb. 3, 1960, when he spoke of "the winds of change" sweeping across the continent. Nigeria, Togo, and Dahomey (Benin) became sovereign states in 1960, Tanganyika (Tanzania), Uganda, and Kenya in East Africa between 1961 and 1963, and Malawi and Northern Rhodesia (Zambia) in the south in 1964. White residents of Southern Rhodesia, however, declared their own indepen-dence in defiance of London and the UN. The Republic of South Africa and the surviving Portuguese colonies of Angola and Mozambique made those portions of southern Africa the last refuges of white rule on the continent.

Most new African states had little more to support their pretensions to nationhood than a paper constitution, a flag, and a London-backed currency. The leaderships blamed African underdevelopment on past exploitation rather than on objective conditions, thus rejecting the American and European development theories that saw political stability as possible only within the context of economic growth. Nkrumah lectured to his Pan-African Congress in 1963 that "the social and economic development of Africa will come only within the political kingdom, not the other way around." Indeed, Africa's politicians invariably styled themselves as charismatic leaders whose political and even spiritual guidance was the prerequisite for progress. Nkrumah himself seized all power in Ghana and made himself a quasi-divine figure until the army overthrew him in 1966. Togo's government fell to a military coup in 1963, and mutinies broke out in Kenya, Uganda, and Tanganyika. In the latter country, Julius Nyerere, much admired in Europe and the United States, declared a one-party dictatorship based on his ideology of *ujamaa* (familyhood) and courted aid from Communist

A youthful Julius Nyerere celebrates Tanzania's forthcoming independence in December 1961.

China. Other leaders contrived similar ideologies to justify personal rule. By 1967 black Africa had suffered 64 attempted coups d'état, many born of tribal hatreds, and most Africans had fewer political rights than under colonial rule.

With the exception of Congo (Brazzaville), Cold War rivalries were absent from Africa in the 1960s, while the African regimes themselves wisely declared the inviolability of their boundaries lest the artificial lines drawn by the colonial powers provoke endless warfare. When Igbo tribes-people seceded from Nigeria in 1967 and formed the rebel state of Biafra, only four African nations supported their cause. Nigeria suppressed the secession in a bloody civil war. Decolonization nonetheless had a profound effect on international relations through the medium of the UN. The three dozen or so new African states combined with those of Asia and the Soviet bloc to form a permanent majority made up mostly of one-party dictatorships nevertheless claiming moral superiority over the Western "imperialists." Thus, the founders' dreams that the UN might become a "parliament of the world" and bulwark of democracy and human rights were undermined by the very process of what, with one or another degree of irony, was called "liberation." Instead, the UN degenerated into a forum for polemics and a playground for intrigue.

FRANCE'S INDEPENDENT COURSE

Where Britain was enervated by the advent of the missile age and the Third World, France was invigorated. The weak Fourth Republic had suffered defeat in Indochina and was embroiled in a civil war between French settlers and native Muslims in Algeria. When de Gaulle was called back to power eight months after Sputnik 1, he set about to forestall a threatened coup d'état by the French army, stabilize French politics, end the Algerian debacle (independence was granted in 1962 in the Treaty of Évian), and restore French power and prestige in the world. His constitution for a Fifth Republic established presidential leadership and restored France's political stability, itself an achievement of great value to the West. De Gaulle's vision of France, however, involved neither *la plus grande France* of the colonial empire nor the Atlanticist France of NATO nor the European France of the Common Market (EEC). Rather, de Gaulle proclaimed that a France without grandeur was not France at all and set out to reestablish French military, technological, and diplomatic independence.

France's decolonization proceeded as rapidly as Britain's, culminating in 1960 with the partition and independence of French West Africa into the nations of Guinea, Mali (formerly French Sudan), Senegal, and Upper Volta (which changed its name to Burkina Faso in 1984). De Gaulle, however, refused to exhibit any guilt or doubt about France's *mission civilisatrice* and offered the populations a choice between going it alone or joining a linguistic, monetary, and development community with the former metropole. Only Guinea elected to follow a Marxist leader who sought ties with the U.S.S.R.

In defense matters, de Gaulle bristled at NATO's reliance on the United States and publicly doubted whether the U.S. nuclear umbrella over Europe was still reliable after Sputnik. Would the Americans really risk a nuclear attack on New York City or Washington, D.C., to defend Berlin or Paris? Therefore, de Gaulle accelerated the quiet development of a nuclear capacity begun under the Fourth Republic, and France exploded its first atomic bomb in 1960. He also quintupled French spending on research and development, built independent bomber, missile, and submarine forces—the nuclear *force de frappe*—and made France the third space power with the launch of an Earth satellite in 1965.

Gaullist France's rebellion against the tutelage of a superpower unwilling to accord it diplomatic equality or help it develop nuclear weapons bore genuine comparison to Maoist China. Like the U.S.S.R., the United States tried various means to rein in its obstreperous ally, first trying to dissuade France from developing nuclear weapons, then inviting it to join a multilateral nuclear force (MLF) under NATO command. First suggested in December 1960, the MLF was pushed by Kennedy and Johnson, but de Gaulle responded with contempt, while Adenauer feared to join lest he damage West German relations with France. The idea of an MLF died in 1965, and in July 1966 de Gaulle took the final step of withdrawing French armed forces from NATO (though France remained a political member of the alliance). NATO headquarters were then moved from Paris to Brussels.

De Gaulle similarly distrusted the movement for European integration, preferring what he termed "the Europe of the fatherlands" stretching "from the Atlantic to the Urals"—the latter phrase provocatively including the European portion of the Soviet Union. He tolerated European institutions such as the EEC, but only on terms of strict French leadership in partnership with West Germany; hence his veto of Britain's application in 1963. Moreover, de Gaulle viewed European cooperative programs in atomic and space research as ways to tap foreign contributions for the improvement of French national competitiveness, not as ways for France to contribute to European unity. Adenauer eagerly accepted de Gaulle's leadership in order to complete Germany's postwar rehabilitation and retain the EEC market for Germany's booming industry. De Gaulle, however, crushed any lingering hopes for European political integration by boycotting the EEC in 1965–66 rather than allow the federalist commissioner Walter Hallstein to enhance the decision-making power of the EEC Parliament. Finally, de Gaulle delighted in open criticism of American foreign policy and courted closer relations with Moscow (which in return seized upon what appeared to be an opportunity to split the alliance), culminating in the pomp of a state visit in 1966. In all these ways Gaullist policy was a constant vexation to Washington, but in the long run it was probably a boon to the Western alliance for the technological dynamism, political stability, and military might it restored to France.

CHAPTER 4

ASIA BENEATH THE SUPERPOWERS

The first rebellions against the European imperial system had occurred on the rimlands of Asia at the start of the 20th century: the Russo-Japanese War, the Indian home-rule movement, and the Chinese and Young Turk revolutions. By the 1960s the southern tier of Asian states had given birth to local systems of power and rivalry beyond the control of the Great Powers. Several factors set these nations and their conflicts apart. First, the Middle East, the Indian subcontinent, and Indochina all seethed with ethnic conflicts that had little to do with the Cold War. Second, eastern and southern Asia continued to undergo a demographic explosion that made China and India by far the most populous states in the world and non-Soviet Asia the home of 55 percent of the human race. Third, the politics of these societies, involved as they were in the awakening of vast peasant masses, the breakdown of traditional village agriculture, religious and dynastic structures, and programs for rapid modernization, did not easily fall into categories familiar to Soviet and American planners of the 1950s. Fourth, most of the Asian rim was remote from the European Soviet Union and North America, making direct intervention there expensive and risky.

Nevertheless, continued Soviet efforts to win influence in the Middle East, Chinese claims to natural leadership of the poor southern half of the globe, and American attempts to preserve a structure of containment of the Communist world necessarily involved the Great Powers in Asian diplomacy. The fate of half of mankind could not, it seemed, be a matter of indifference to countries that claimed universal missions.

By 1972 the U.S.S.R., despite its achievement of relative parity in nuclear weapons, was obsessed with the prospect of a hostile China, while the United States, having squandered its wealth, prestige, and domestic tranquillity in the Vietnam War, was trying to scale back its global commitments. The Nixon Doctrine, détente with Moscow, the opening to China, and uncoupling of the dollar from gold were the symptoms of this American retreat.

The Six-Day War

In the Middle East, Nasser's star began to decline in the 1960s from its post-Suez peak. The Syrian Ba'th Party, though social-ist, resented Nasser's assumption of Arab leadership and in 1961 took the country out of the United Arab Republic, which it had formed with Egypt in 1958. Likewise, the presence of 50,000 Egyptian troops in Yemen failed to overcome the forces supporting the Yemeni imam, who was backed in turn by Saudi Arabia. On the other hand, the Cairo Conference of 1964 suc-ceeded in rallying pan-Arab unity around resistance to Israel's plans to divert the waters of the Jordan. Also with both eyes on Israel, the conference restored an Arab High Command and elevated the Palestinian refugees (scattered among several Arab states since 1948) to a status approaching sovereignty, with their own army and headquarters in the Gaza Strip. Syria likewise sponsored a terrorist organization, al-Fatah, whose raids against Jewish settlements provoked Israeli military repri-sals inside Jordan and Lebanon. Syria was divided principally between the socialist Ba'th, led by the minority 'Alawite com-munity that dominated the army, and pro-Nasser pan-Arabists.

In 1966 a military coup established a radical Ba'thist regime, but the army itself then split into rival factions. Nasser took the initiative to prevent a rightist reversal in Syria and reassert his leadership of the Arab cause.

Armed with Soviet tanks and planes, Nasser claimed his option under the 1956 accord to demand withdrawal of UN peacekeeping forces from the Sinai. Secretary-General U Thant complied on May 19, 1967. Four days later Nasser closed the Gulf of Aqaba to Israeli shipping. The Soviets apparently urged Nasser to show moderation, while President Johnson told Israeli Foreign Minister Abba Eban to remain calm: "Israel will not be alone unless it decides to go alone." Neither superpower, however, was able to restrain its client.

When Egyptian and Iraqi troops arrived in Jordan, giving every sign of an imminent pan-Arab attack, the Israeli Cabinet decided on a preemptive strike. On the morning of June 5, the

An Israeli armoured troop unit enters Gaza during the Six-Day War on June 6, 1967.

Israeli air force destroyed Nasser's planes on the ground. Without cover from the air, the Egyptian army was left vulnerable to attack. Within three days the Israelis had achieved an overwhelming victory on the ground, capturing the Gaza Strip and all of the Sinai Peninsula up to the east bank of the Suez Canal. On June 7 Israeli forces drove Jordanian forces out of East Jerusalem and most of the West Bank. The UN Security Council called for a cease-fire on June 7 that was immediately accepted by Israel and Jordan. Egypt accepted the following day. Syria held out, however, and continued to shell villages in northern Israel. On June 9 Israel launched an assault on the fortified Golan Heights, capturing it from Syrian forces after a day of heavy fighting. Syria accepted the cease-fire on June 10.

The Israelis were willing to view their conquests (except Jerusalem) as bargaining chips but insisted on Arab recognition of the right of Israel to exist and firm guarantees against future attack. The so-called frontline Arab states were neither able (for domestic reasons) nor willing to give such guarantees and instead courted Soviet and Third World support against "U.S.–Israeli imperialism." Hence Israel remained both greatly enlarged and possessed of shorter, more defensible borders, although it did acquire the problem of administering more than a million Arabs in Gaza and the West Bank. Going forward, the status of Palestinians living in the occupied territories under Israeli rule became a major sticking point in the Arab-Israeli wars.

The Arab countries' losses in the Six-Day War were disastrous. Egypt's casualties numbered more than 11,000, with 6,000 for Jordan and 1,000 for Syria, compared with only 700 for Israel. The Arab armies also suffered crippling losses of weaponry and equipment. The lopsidedness of the defeat demoralized both the Arab public and the political elite. Nasser announced his resignation on June 9 but quickly yielded to mass demonstrations calling for him to remain in office. In Israel, which had proved beyond question that it was the region's preeminent military power, there was euphoria.

China, India, and Pakistan

The Indian subcontinent comprised another system of conflict focused on border disputes among India, Pakistan, and China. Jawaharlal Nehru's Congress Party had stabilized the political life of the teeming and disparate peoples of India. The United States looked to India as a laboratory of democracy and development in the Third World and a critical foil to Communist China and in consequence had contributed substantial amounts of aid. The U.S.S.R. also began an effective aid program in 1955, and Nehru looked to the U.S.S.R. for support against China once the Sino-Soviet split became evident. The Peking regime had brutally suppressed the buffer state of Tibet in 1950 and disputed the border with India at several points between the tiny Himalayan states of Nepal, Bhutan, and Sikkim. American military aid to Pakistan (a member of CENTO) also gave the Indians and Soviets reason to cooperate. In 1961, when President Ayub Khan of Pakistan earnestly sought Kennedy's mediation in the dispute over Kashmir, U.S. pressure proved inadequate to bring Nehru to the bargaining table.

Nehru was humbled, however, when the Chinese suddenly attacked in force across the disputed boundaries, choosing as their moment the height of the Cuban missile crisis. Indian forces were soundly defeated, 7,000 men having been killed or captured, and the lowlands of Assam lay open to the invaders. The Chinese leadership apparently had expected a Soviet triumph in Cuba, or at least a drawn-out crisis that would prevent superpower intervention in India, but the swift resolution in Cuba in favour of the United States permitted Washington to respond to Nehru's request for help. The Chinese then halted the offensive and soon afterward withdrew.

The Kennedy administration used its newly won leverage to urge Nehru to settle his quarrel with Pakistan, but the negotiations failed to overcome Hindu–Muslim antipathy and the fact that the conflict was a unifying element in the domestic politics of both countries. Pakistani troops crossed the cease-fire line in Kashmir in August 1965, and India responded by invading Pakistan proper. Both superpowers backed U Thant's personal quest for a cease-fire, and the Indians withdrew. The U.S.S.R. was able to regain influence with New Delhi, especially after the accession to power of Nehru's daughter, Indira Gandhi. In 1971 India and the U.S.S.R. concluded a 20-year Treaty of Peace and Friendship and Cooperation, an indication of how much the United States (not to mention Britain) had lost touch with the once model Third World democracy.

Indira Gandhi was prime minister of India from 1980 until 1984.

Pakistan, meanwhile, was in ferment. President Ayub Khan was forced to step down in 1969 in favour of Yahya Khan, while elections in 1970 polarized the geographically divided country. West Pakistan chose Zulfikar Ali Bhutto as prime minister, but densely populated East Pakistan (Bengal) voted almost unanimously for a separatist party under Mujibur Rahman. When talks between the two leaders broke down, Bhutto gambled on sending in troops and jailing the secessionists. Vicious fighting broke out in Bengal, flooding India with some 10,000,000 refugees and provoking Indian intervention. The Soviets cautioned restraint but clearly favoured India, while U.S. President Nixon sent a carrier task force into the Bay of Bengal and openly favoured Pakistan, influenced by the country's role as intermediary between Washington and Peking. In two weeks of fighting (Dec. 3–16, 1971) the Indians defeated the Pakistanis on all fronts, and East Pakistan became the new state of Bangladesh, comprising the delta of the Indus River. Pakistan thus lost well over half its population. Once Nixon's opening to China bore fruit, the subcontinent seemed to be polarized around a U.S.S.R.–India axis and a U.S.–Pakistan–China axis, though the United States resumed aid and food shipments during the Indian famine of 1972.

To the south and east of the Asian mainland lay the vast, populous archipelago of Indonesia, where another romantic revolutionary, Sukarno, had played host to the Bandung Conference of 1955. Like Nasser, Nehru, and Mao, he ruled his 100,000,000 people by vague, moralizing slogans that added up to a personal ideology with nationalist and Communist overtones. The Kennedy administration had tried to appease Sukarno with development aid and even obliged the Dutch to cede Irian Barat (Irian Jaya) in the face of Sukarno's threats in 1963. Sukarno still turned to Moscow for support and gave himself over to degenerate personal behaviour and foreign adventures, most notably an attempted attack on Malaysia in 1963. By 1965 Indonesia was $2,400,000,000 in debt and suffering widespread famine. In January of that year Sukarno withdrew his country from the UN over a dispute with Malaysia. The Soviets were clearly disgusted with Sukarno's regime, while the rival Chinese persuaded (perhaps blackmailed) him into approving a savage pro-Communist putsch in October 1965. Suharto, however, put down the uprising and exacted a violent revenge in which as many as 300,000 Communists and their supporters were killed. Indonesia subsequently concerned itself with its internal problems, frustrating Soviet, Chinese, and American hopes for a strong ally.

The destruction of Indonesian Communism, achieved without the slightest American effort, was a source of great comfort for the United States. A diametrically opposite course of events had, by 1965, begun to unfold in the last theatre of Asian conflict, Vietnam.

The Vietnam War

As the Vietnam War began to recede into the past, the entire episode, from a neutral perspective, increasingly came to seem incredible. That the most powerful and wealthy nation on earth should undertake 15 years of wasting conflict against a tiny state 10,000 miles from its shores—and lose—almost justifies the historian Paul Johnson's phrase "America's suicide attempt." Yet the destructive and futile U.S. engagement in Southeast Asia was a product of a series of trends that had been maturing since World War II.

The early Cold War gave rise to U.S. leadership in the containment of Communism. Decolonization then thrust the United States into a role described by advocate and critic alike as "the world's policeman"—protector and benefactor of the weak new governments of the Third World. The potential of guerrilla insurgency, demonstrated in Tito's resistance to the Nazis and especially in the postwar victories of Mao, the Viet Minh, and Castro, made it the preferred mode for revolutionary action around the world. The emerging nuclear stalemate alerted Washington to the need to prepare for fighting limited (sometimes called "brushfire") wars sponsored by the Soviet Union or China through proxies in the Third World. In this era of Khrushchevian and Maoist assertiveness the United States could not allow any of its client states to fall to a Communist "war of national liberation" lest it lose prestige and credibility to Moscow and Peking. Finally, the "domino theory," that the fall of one country would inexorably lead to the communization of its neighbours, magnified the importance of even the smallest state and guaranteed that sooner or later the United States would become entangled under the worst possible conditions. One or even all of the assumptions under which the United States became involved in Vietnam may have been faulty, but very few in the government and the public questioned them until long after the country was committed.

THE U.S. ENTERS THE WAR

By 1961, Diem's fledgling government in South Vietnam was receiving more U.S. aid per capita than any other country except Laos and South Korea. Authoritative reports detailed both the Viet Cong's campaign of terror against government officials in the south and widespread discontent over Diem's corrupt and imperious rule. In the face of both Khrushchev's renewed vow to support wars of national liberation and de Gaulle's warning ("I predict you will sink step by step into a bottomless military and political quagmire"), Kennedy chose Vietnam as a test case for American theories of state building and counterinsurgency. He approved a proposal by Rostow and General Maxwell Taylor to assign advisers to every level of Saigon's government and military, and the number of Americans in Vietnam grew from 800 to 11,000 by the end of 1962.

Ho Chi Minh's North Vietnamese considered the struggle against Diem and his American sponsors merely the next phase of a war that had begun against the Japanese and had continued against the French. Their determination to unify Vietnam and conquer all of Indochina was the principal dynamic behind the conflict. The total number of Communist troops in the South grew by recruitment and infiltration from some 7,000 in 1960 to more than 100,000 by 1964. Most were guerrilla militiamen who served also as local party cadres. Above them were the Viet Cong (formally the National Liberation Front, or NLF), deployed in regional military units, and units of the People's Army of North Vietnam (PAVN) entering the South along the Ho Chi Minh Trail. U.S. Special Forces tried to counter Communist control of the countryside with a "strategic hamlet" program, a tactic used with success by the British in Malaya. Diem instituted a policy of relocating the rural population of South Vietnam in order to isolate the Communists. The program caused widespread resentment, while Diem's persecution of local Buddhist sects provided a rallying point for protests. When Buddhist monks resorted to dramatic self-immolation in front of Western news cameras, Kennedy secretly instructed Ambassador Henry Cabot Lodge to approve a military coup. On Nov. 1, 1963, Diem was overthrown and murdered.

South Vietnam then underwent a succession of coups d'état that undermined all pretense that the United States was defending democracy. The struggle was thenceforth viewed in Washington as a military effort to buy time for state building and the training of the South Vietnamese army (Army of the Republic of Vietnam; ARVN). When two American destroyers exchanged fire with a North Vietnamese torpedo boat eight miles off the North's coast in August 1964 (an event whose occurrence was later disputed), Congress passed the Gulf of Tonkin Resolution authorizing the President to take whatever measures he deemed necessary to protect American lives in Southeast Asia. Johnson held off escalating the war during the 1964 electoral campaign, but in February 1965 he ordered sustained bombing of North Vietnam and sent the first U.S. combat units to the South. By June, U.S. troops in Vietnam numbered 74,000.

The Soviet Union reacted to American escalation by trying to reconvene the Geneva Conference and bring pressure to bear on the United States to submit to the peaceful reunification of Vietnam. China bluntly refused to encourage a negotiated settlement and insisted that the U.S.S.R. help North Vietnam by pressuring the United States elsewhere. The Soviets, in turn, resented Peking's assertion of leadership in the Communist world and had no desire to provoke new crises with Washington. The North Vietnamese were caught in the middle; Ho's ties were to Moscow, but geography obliged him to favour Peking. Hence North Vietnam joined in boycotting the March 1965 Communist conference in Moscow. The Soviets, however, dared not ignore the Vietnam War lest they confirm Chinese accusations of Soviet "revisionism."

THE CONDUCT AND COST OF THE WAR

Meanwhile, the United States slid inevitably into the quagmire predicted by de Gaulle. U.S. forces reached a peak of 543,000 men in 1969. (Australia, New Zealand, Thailand, and the Philippines also sent small contingents, and South Korea contributed 50,000 men.) The U.S. strategy was to employ mobility, based on helicopters, and firepower to wear down the enemy by attrition at minimal cost in U.S. lives.

The war of attrition on the ground, like the bombing in the North, was designed less to destroy the enemy's ability to wage war than to demonstrate to the enemy that he could not win and to bring him to the bargaining table. But stalemate suited Hanoi, which could afford to wait, while it was anathema to the Americans. Johnson's popularity fell steadily. Most Americans favoured more vigorous prosecution to end the war, but a growing number advocated withdrawal. Antiwar dissent grew and spread and overlapped with sweeping and violent demands for social change. Vietnam shattered the American foreign policy consensus that had sustained containment since the 1940s. In retrospect, Johnson's attempt to prevent the war from disturbing his own domestic program was vain, and his strategic conception was grounded in folly and hubris. He and his advisers had no clear notion of what the application of American force was supposed to achieve. It was merely assumed to be invincible.

Hanoi understood that the classic Maoist strategy of isolating cities by revolutionizing the countryside was inapplicable to Vietnam because the cities could still hold out with foreign support. Accordingly, in mid-1967 the North Vietnamese Politburo approved a plan for urban attacks throughout South Vietnam. General Vo Nguyen Giap insisted, however, that NLF guerrillas, not PAVN units, be risked. The expectation was that direct attacks on cities would undercut American claims of pacification and magnify domestic American dissent. On Jan. 30, 1968 (the Tet holiday, during which many ARVN troops were home on leave), an estimated 84,000 Communist troops infiltrated South Vietnamese cities, attacked government installations, and even penetrated the American embassy in Saigon. The Tet Offensive was carried out at a terrible cost to Communist strength, but American press reports turned the offensive into a psychological defeat for the United States.

Instead of ordering a counterattack, Johnson removed himself from the 1968 presidential campaign, ordered a bombing halt, and pledged to devote the rest of his administration to the quest for peace. Negotiations began in Paris, but the rest of the year was spent bickering over procedural issues.

For more than 25 years after 1941 the United States had maintained an unprecedented depth of involvement in world affairs. In 1968 Vietnam finally forced Americans to face the limits of their resources and will. Whoever succeeded Johnson would have little choice but to find a way to escape from Vietnam and reduce American global responsibilities.

Nixon, Kissinger, and Détente

After eight years in the shadow of Eisenhower and eight more years out of office, Richard Nixon brought to the presidency in 1969 rich experience as an observer of foreign affairs and shrewd notions about how to prevent the American retreat from global commitments from turning into a rout. In broad outlines, the Nixon strategy included a phased withdrawal of ground forces from Vietnam, a negotiated settlement saving the Saigon regime, détente with the U.S.S.R., resumption of relations with mainland China, and military support for selected regional powers that permitted them to take over as local "policemen" in lieu of direct American involvement.

In a period of just four years, 1969–72, the United States abandoned once-unshakable Cold War attitudes toward the Communist nations, while scaling back its own exposure in response to the Sino-Soviet split, imminent Soviet strategic parity, and the economic and psychological constraints on U.S. action stemming from the new American imperative of "no more Vietnams." Nixon believed that his own record as an anti-Communist and tough negotiator would quiet conservative opposition to détente, while liberals would find themselves outflanked on their own peace issue. In both ends and means American foreign policy demonstrated a new realism in stark contrast to the "pay any price, bear any burden" mentality of the Kennedy–Johnson years. In his inaugural address Nixon spoke instead of an "era of negotiation."

THE ERA OF NEGOTIATION

Détente, however, was not meant to replace the abiding post-war American strategy of containment. Rather, it was meant to be a less confrontational method of containing Communist power through diplomatic accords and a flexible system of rewards and punishments by which Washington might moderate Soviet behaviour. Journalists dubbed this tactic "linkage" insofar as the United States would link positive inducements (*e.g.,* arms control, technology transfers, grain sales) to expected Soviet reciprocity in other areas (*e.g.,* restraint in promoting revolutionary movements). Nixon had no illusions that U.S.–Soviet competition would disappear, but he expected that this carrot-and-stick approach would establish rules of the game and recognized spheres of influence. Pulling the Soviets into a network of agreements, and thus giving them a stake in the status quo, would create a stable structure of peace. Finally, expanding economic and cultural ties might even serve to open up Soviet society.

By 1971, Leonid Brezhnev, now established as the new Soviet leader, was ready to welcome American overtures for a variety of reasons. In 1968 relations with the eastern European satellites had flared up again when leaders of the Czechoslovakian Communist party under Alexander Dubček initiated reforms promoting democratization and free speech. A wave of popular demonstrations added momentum to liberalization

PRAGUE SPRING

Prague Spring was a brief period of liberalization in Czechoslovakia under Alexander Dubček in 1968. Soon after he became first secretary of the Czechoslovak Communist Party on Jan. 5, 1968, Dubček granted the press greater freedom of expression; he also rehabilitated victims of political purges during the Joseph Stalin era.

The crown achievement of the new reformist government was the Action Program, adopted by the party's Central Committee in April 1968. The program encompassed not only economic reforms but also the democratization of Czechoslovak political life. Among its most important points were the promotion of Slovakia to full parity within a new Czechoslovak federation, long overdue industrial and agricultural reforms, and a revised constitution that would guarantee civil rights and liberties. Political pluralism was not recommended, but the Communist Party would have to justify its leading role by competing freely for supremacy with other organizations in the process of formation. International opinion saw Dubček as offering "socialism with a human face."

The effect of the liberalization movement on the Czechoslovak public was unprecedented and quite unexpected. Alternative forms of political organization quickly emerged. Former political prisoners founded K 231, a group named after the article of the criminal code under which they had been sentenced; a number of prominent intellectuals formed KAN, a club for committed non-Communist Party members; and there even were efforts to reestablish the Social Democratic Party, forcibly fused with the Communist Party in 1948. With the collapse of the official communist youth movement, youth clubs and the Boy Scouts were resurrected. Christian churches, national minority associations, human rights groups, and other long-forgotten societies became active as well.

On June 27, 1968, the dissident writer Ludvík Vaculík published a document signed by a large number of people representing all walks of Czechoslovak life. This document, dubbed the "Two Thousand Words" manifesto, constituted a watershed in the evolution of the Prague Spring: it urged mass action to demand real democracy. Though shocked by the proclamation, Dubček was convinced that he could control the transformation of Czechoslovakia.

The Soviet Union and the other Warsaw Pact allies were far more alarmed. After Dubček declined to participate in a special meeting of the Warsaw Pact powers, they sent him a letter on July 15 saying that his country was on the verge of counterrevolution and that they considered it their duty to protect it. Nevertheless, Dubček remained confident that he could talk himself out of any difficulties with his fellow communist leaders.

However, on the evening of Aug. 20, 1968, Soviet-led armed forces invaded the country. The Soviet authorities seized Dubček, Oldřich Černík, and several other leaders and secretly took them to Moscow. Meanwhile, the population spontaneously reacted against the invasion through acts of passive resistance and improvisation (*e.g.*, road signs were removed so that the invading troops would get lost). But by August 27 the Czechoslovaks had been compelled to yield to the Soviets' demands in an agreement known as the Moscow Protocol. Svoboda, bringing with him Dubček and the other leaders, returned to Prague to tell the population what price they would have to pay for their "socialism with a human face": Soviet troops were going to stay in Czechoslovakia for the time being, and the leaders had agreed to tighter controls over political and cultural activities.

The continued presence of Soviet troops helped the communist hard-liners, who were joined by Husák, to defeat Dubček and the reformers. On April 17, 1969, Dubček was replaced as first secretary.

during this "Prague Spring" until, on August 20, the U.S.S.R. led neighbouring Warsaw Pact armies in a military invasion of Czechoslovakia. Dubček was ousted and the reforms undone.

The ostensible justification for this latest Soviet

repression of freedom in its empire came to be known as the Brezhnev Doctrine: "Each of our parties is responsible not only to its working class and its people, but also to the international working class, the world Communist movement." The U.S.S.R. asserted its right to intervene in any Communist state to prevent the success of "counterrevolutionary" elements. Needless to say, the Chinese were fearful that the Brezhnev Doctrine might be applied to them. In 1969 they accused the U.S.S.R. of "social imperialism" and provoked hundreds of armed clashes on the borders of Sinkiang and Manchuria. Soviet forces arrayed against China, already raised from 12 weak divisions in 1961 to 25 full ones, now grew to 55 divisions backed by 120 SS-11 nuclear missiles. In August 1969 a Soviet diplomat had carefully inquired about the likely American reaction to a Soviet nuclear strike against China. In sum, the need to repair the Soviet image in the wake of the Prague Spring and the fear of dangerous relations with Peking and Washington at the same time, as well as the chronic Soviet need for agricultural imports and access to superior Western technology, were all powerful incentives for seeking détente.

From a longer perspective, however, détente had been the strategy of the U.S.S.R. ever since 1956 under the rubric "peaceful coexistence." Brezhnev repeated Khrushchev's assertion that Soviet nuclear parity took the military leverage from the hands of the bourgeois world, forcing it to accept the legitimate interests of other states, to treat the U.S.S.R. as an equal, and to acquiesce in the success of "progressive" and revolutionary struggle. Détente was thus for the Soviets a natural expression of the new correlation of forces, a means of guiding the weakened Americans through the transition to a new phase of history—and was certainly not meant to preserve the status quo or liberalize the U.S.S.R. One Western proponent of détente described the Soviet conception of it as a way "to make the world safe for historical change" and pointed out the implicit double standard—*i.e.,* that it was admissible for the U.S.S.R. to continue the struggle against the capitalist world during détente but a contradiction for the Western powers to struggle against Communism. From the Marxist point of view, however, this was merely another reflection of objective reality: Now that nuclear balance was a fact, greater weight was given to conventional military strength and popular political action, each of which strongly favoured the Socialist bloc.

The contrasting U.S. and Soviet conceptions of détente would eventually scuttle the hopes placed in it on both sides. From 1969 to 1972, however, those differences were not yet apparent, while the immediate incentives for a relaxation of tensions were irresistible.

SCALING BACK U.S. COMMITMENTS

The first indications of a new American sense of limits in foreign policy were in the economic sphere. Since World War II the global market economy had rested on the Bretton Woods monetary system, based on a strong American dollar tied to gold. Beginning in 1958 the United States began to run annual foreign-exchange deficits, resulting partly from the costs of maintaining U.S. forces overseas. For this reason, and because their own exports benefitted from an artificially strong dollar, the Europeans and Japanese tolerated the U.S. gold drain and used their growing fund of "Eurodollars" to back loans and commerce. By the mid-1960s de Gaulle began to criticize the United States for exploiting its leadership role to "export its inflation" to foreign holders of dollars. The Johnson administration's Vietnam deficits then added the prospect of internal American inflation.

By 1971 the American economic situation warranted

emergency measures. Nixon imposed wage and price controls to stem inflation, and Secretary of the Treasury John Connally abruptly suspended the convertibility of dollars to gold. The dollar was allowed to float against undervalued currencies like the deutsche mark and yen, in consequence of which foreign holders of dollars took sharp losses and foreign exporters faced stiffer competition from American goods. New agreements in December 1971 stabilized the dollar at a rate 12 percent below Bretton Woods, but the United States had sorely tried allied loyalty.

The American retreat from an overextended financial position and insistence that its allies share the burden of stabilizing the U.S. balance of payments was the economic analog to the Nixon Doctrine in military affairs. The new president enunciated this doctrine in an impromptu news conference on Guam during his July 1969 trip to welcome home the Apollo 11 astronauts from the Moon. Nixon announced that the United States would no longer send Americans to fight for Asian nations but would confine itself to logistical and economic support: "Asian hands must shape the Asian future." In accord with this effort to shift more of the burden of containment to threatened peoples themselves, Nixon planned to assist regional pro-Western powers like Iran in becoming bulwarks of stability by providing them with sophisticated American weapons.

Before the Nixon Doctrine could be credible, however, the president had to extricate the United States from Vietnam. In March 1969 he outlined a policy of Vietnamization, comprising a phased withdrawal of American ground troops and additional material and advisory support to make the ARVN self-sufficient. Nixon also hoped to enlist the Soviets in the cause of peace, but Moscow had less influence over Hanoi than he imagined and could not afford to be seen as appeasing the United States. Nixon then shifted to a subtler approach—long-term pressure on Hanoi combined with better relations with both Communist giants. Late in 1969 secret talks began in Paris between Henry Kissinger, Nixon's adviser for national security, and the North Vietnamese Politburo member Le Duc Tho. At the same time, however, Nixon stepped up pressure on the North. When the anti-Communist general Lon Nol overthrew Prince Sihanouk in Cambodia in March 1970, Nixon acceded to the U.S. army's long-standing desire to destroy Communist sanctuaries inside that country. The U.S.-ARVN operation fell short of its promise and provoked protests at home and abroad. Despite public disfavour and congressional attempts to limit such actions, Nixon ordered continued secret American bombing inside Cambodia and also supported an ARVN operation into Laos to cut the Ho Chi Minh Trail.

THE OPENING TO CHINA AND *OSTPOLITIK*

The linchpin of Nixon's strategy for a settlement in Vietnam was détente with Moscow and Peking. He was known as a firm supporter of the Nationalist regime on Taiwan, but he had softened his stance against mainland China before taking office. In 1969 he moved to signal Peking through the good offices of de Gaulle and Yahya Khan of Pakistan. Direct contacts, conducted through the Chinese embassy in Warsaw, were broken off after the 1970 U.S.-ARVN attacks on Cambodia, but Nixon and Kissinger remained hopeful. The Cultural Revolution ended in a serious power struggle in the Chinese leadership. Army commander Lin Biao opposed relations with the United States but died when his plane crashed in unclear circumstances. Chinese premier Zhou Enlai and Mao (presumably) contemplated the value of an American counterweight to the Soviets, concessions on the status of Taiwan, and technology transfers. The Nixon Doctrine also promised to remove the obnoxious U.S. military presence in Asia.

The Pakistani channel bore fruit in December 1970, when

Yahya Khan returned from Peking with an invitation for an American envoy to discuss Taiwan. The following April the Chinese made the surprising public gesture of inviting an American table tennis team to the championship tournament in Peking. This episode of "Ping-Pong diplomacy" was followed by a secret trip to Peking by Kissinger. Kissinger's talks with Zhou and Mao yielded an American promise to remove U.S. forces from Taiwan in return for Chinese support of a negotiated settlement in Vietnam. The Chinese also agreed to a presidential visit in February 1972. The American people's long-latent fascination with China immediately revived, and Nixon's trip was a sensation.

The Soviets watched with palpable discomfort as Nixon and Mao embraced and saluted each other's flags, and they quickly raised the premium on improving relations with Washington. Efforts to this end had been frustrated by a series of crises: a

Zhou Enlai (center left) *and Richard Nixon* (center right) *during Nixon's historic visit to China in February 1972.*

buildup of Soviet jets in Egypt and Jordan, the discovery of a Soviet submarine base under construction in Cuba in 1970, and Nixon's escalations of the war in Southeast Asia. Substantial moves toward East–West détente had already been made in Europe, however. Following de Gaulle's lead, the West German foreign minister, Willy Brandt, a Socialist and former mayor of West Berlin, had made overtures toward Moscow. After becoming chancellor in 1969 he pursued a thorough *Ostpolitik* ("eastern policy") that culminated in treaties with the U.S.S.R. (August 1970), renouncing the use of force in their relations, and with Poland (December 1970), recognizing Germany's 1945 losses east of the Oder–Neisse Line. Brandt also recognized the East German government (December 1972) and expanded commercial relations with other eastern European regimes. Both German states were admitted to the UN in 1973. Support for *Ostpolitik* among West Germans reflected the growing belief that German reunification would more likely be achieved through détente, rather than confrontation, with the Soviet bloc.

The United States, Britain, and France seconded Brandt's efforts by concluding a new Four Power accord with the U.S.S.R. on Berlin in September 1971. The Soviets made what they considered a major concession by agreeing to retain their responsibility under the Potsdam Accords for access to West Berlin and achieved in return Western recognition of the status quo in eastern Europe and access to West German technology and credits.

ARMS-LIMITATION NEGOTIATIONS

The centrepiece of a bilateral U.S.–Soviet détente, however, had to be the Strategic Arms Limitation Talks (SALT), which began in 1969. After a decade of determined research and deployment the Soviet Union had pulled ahead of the United States in long-range missiles and was catching up in submarine-launched missiles and in long-range bombers. Indeed, it had been American policy since the mid-1960s to permit the Soviets to achieve parity in order to stabilize the regime of mutual deterrence. Stability was threatened, however, from the technological quarter with the development of multiple independently targeted reentry vehicles (MIRVs), by which several warheads, each aimed at a different target, could be carried on one missile, and antiballistic missiles (ABMs), which might allow one side to strike first while shielding itself from retaliation. In the arcane province of strategic theory, therefore, offense (long-range missiles) became defense, and defense (ABM) offense.

Johnson had favoured a thin ABM system to protect the United States from a Chinese attack, and in 1969 Nixon won Senate approval of ABM deployment by a single vote. He intended, however, to use the program as a bargaining chip. The Soviets had actually deployed a rudimentary ABM system but were anxious to halt the U.S. program before superior American technology left theirs behind. The public SALT talks stalled, but back-channel negotiations between Kissinger and Ambassador Anatoly Dobrynin produced agreement in principle in May 1971 to limit long-range missiles and ABM deployment. The American opening to China made the Soviets increasingly eager for a prompt agreement and summit meeting, while the Americans hoped that Moscow would encourage North Vietnam to be forthcoming in the peace talks.

Since 1968 North Vietnamese negotiators had demanded satisfaction of Premier Pham Van Dong's "four points" of 1965, including cessation of all U.S. military activity in Indochina, termination of foreign military alliances with

Saigon, a coalition government in the South that included the NLF, and reunification of Vietnam. The United States demanded withdrawal of all foreign troops from the South, including the PAVN. This deadlock, plus Hanoi's anxiety over the possible effects of détente, prompted another North Vietnamese bid for victory on the battlefield. In March 1972 they committed 10 of their 13 divisions to a massive offensive. Nixon responded by ordering the resumption of bombing of the North for the first time since 1969 and the mining of the harbour at Haiphong, North Vietnam's major port. The offensive stalled.

Nixon's retaliation against North Vietnam prompted speculation that the U.S.S.R. would cancel the planned summit meeting, but Soviet desire for détente prevailed. Kissinger visited Moscow in April 1972 to work out details on SALT and draft a charter for détente. Nixon instructed him "to emphasize the need for a single standard; we could not accept the proposition that the Soviet Union had the right to support liberation movements throughout the world while insisting on the Brezhnev Doctrine inside the satellite orbit." The Soviets, however, refused to make explicit concessions and defined détente as a means of preventing the inevitable struggle between "progressive" and "reactionary" forces from escalating into war. The result was a vague statement of 12 "basic principles of mutual relations" committing the two parties to peaceful coexistence and normal relations based on "sovereignty, equality, non-interference in internal affairs, and mutual advantage."

Nixon then proceeded to Moscow in May 1972 and signed 10 documents providing for cooperation in economics, science and technology, outer space, medicine, health, and the environment. Most important were the SALT accords: an Interim Agreement limiting ballistic-missile deployment for five years and the ABM Treaty limiting each side to two ABM sites, one protecting the national capital, the other a long-range missile site. The treaty also enjoined the signatories not to interfere with each other's "national technical means of verification," a de facto recognition of each side's space-based reconnaissance satellites.

The preliminary SALT agreement appeared to be a significant achievement, but there was in some ways less to it than met the eye. The treaty mandated controlled increases, not decreases, in the Soviet arsenal, while failing to ban development of cruise missiles, space-based weapons, or the MIRVing of existing launchers by the United States or the U.S.S.R. Thus the superpowers sacrificed the right to defend their attack missiles with ABMs while failing to ensure the stability of mutual deterrence. In sum, the limitation of one sort of nuclear launcher (long-range missiles) did not preclude a continuing arms race in other sorts of launchers or in technological upgrades. To be sure, the mere fact of a U.S.–Soviet agreement seemed of psychological value, but only if both sides were genuinely seeking to reduce arsenals and not simply to maneuver diplomatically for a future advantage. Hence the practical value, or danger, of SALT would be revealed only by superpower behaviour in years to come.

END OF THE VIETNAM WAR

The American achievement of détente with both Moscow and Peking and the failure of North Vietnam's spring 1972 offensive moved both protagonists in that conflict to bargain as well. In October the secret talks in Paris between Kissinger and Le Duc Tho finally produced an agreement on a cease-fire, the release of prisoners of war, evacuation of remaining U.S. forces within 60 days, and political negotiations among all Vietnamese parties. South Vietnam's president, Nguyen Van Thieu, then balked: The plan might indeed allow the Americans to claim "peace with honour" and go home, but it would leave Thieu to deal with the Communists while 100,000 PAVN troops remained in his country. When North Vietnam sought to prevent any last-minute changes by releasing in public the Paris terms, Kissinger was obliged to announce on October 26 that "peace is at hand."

After his landslide reelection a week later—a victory aided by the prospect of peace—Nixon determined to force compliance with the terms on both Vietnamese states. Nixon ordered 11 days of intensive bombing over Hanoi itself (December 18–28) while sending Thieu an ultimatum threatening a separate peace and cessation of U.S. aid if Saigon did not accept the peace terms. The United States

In January 1973 delegations led by Le Duc Tho and Henry Kissinger negotiated the end of U.S. involvement in the Vietnam War.

was castigated worldwide for the "Christmas bombing," but, when talks resumed in January, Hanoi and Saigon quickly came to terms. A Vietnam cease-fire went into effect on Jan. 27, 1973, and the last American soldiers departed on March 29.

Vietnam had been America's longest and most divisive war, and public and congressional opinion flatly opposed any resumption of the agony. The 1973 accords, therefore, were a fig leaf hiding the fact that the United States had just lost its first war despite an estimated expenditure of $155,000,000,000, 7,800,000 tons of bombs (more than all countries dropped in all of World War II), and some 58,000 American lives. Estimates of Vietnamese dead (North and South) totaled more than 2,000,000 soldiers and civilians. In its proportional impact on Vietnamese society, the Vietnam War, 1955–75, was the fourth most severe in the world since 1816.

The end of U.S. involvement in Southeast Asia also brought to a close 15 years of astounding change in world politics that featured the arrival of the space and missile age, the climax of decolonization, the assertions of Maoist China and Gaullist France, the shattering of the myth (fostered by Washington and Moscow alike) of a monolithic Communist world, and the relative decline of American power. In 1969, the very moment when astronauts were setting foot on the Moon to fulfill Kennedy's pledge to prove American superiority, Nixon and Kissinger were struggling to adjust to the new realities and manage a limited American retreat. They succeeded brilliantly in establishing a triangular relationship with Moscow and Peking and appeared to have replaced Cold War with détente. Likewise, they appeared to have escaped from Vietnam and implemented the Nixon Doctrine.

New crises and reversals were in the offing, however, that

would prove that the American decline had not yet been arrested. Given these reversals, détente might be judged as much an exercise in American presumption as the Vietnam War. The U.S.S.R. could not be expected to cease its quest for real values in world competition just because the United States was prepared to acknowledge it as a military equal. Rather, with the United States less able to cope, that very equality opened up new opportunities for Soviet expansion. Khrushchev's boast about the new correlation of forces in the world may have brought the Soviets a series of embarrassments from 1957 to 1962, but a decade later it seemed perversely justified.

CHAPTER 5

PEACE AND CONFLICT IN THE 1970S

Events after the 1960s seemed to suggest that the world was entering an era both of complex interdependence among states and of disintegration of the normative values and institutions by which international behaviour had, to a reliable extent, been made predictable. Perhaps this was not an anomaly, for if modern weapons, communications satellites, and global finance and commerce really had created a "global village," in which the security and well-being of all peoples were interdependent, then by the same token the opportunities had never been greater for ethnic, religious, ideological, or economic differences to spark resentment and conflict among the villagers.

In a world so seemingly out of control, it was perhaps a wonder that politics were not even more violent and anarchic, for the liberal dreams of progress nurtured in the 19th century had surely proved false. The spread of modern technology and economic growth around the world had not necessarily increased the number of societies based on human rights and the rule of law, nor had multilateral institutions like the United Nations or financial and economic interdependence created a higher unity and common purpose among nations, except within the durable and democratic North Atlantic alliance.

Instead, the world after the 1960s saw a proliferation of violence at every level except war among developed nations, a world financial structure under tremendous strain, the worst economic downturn since the 1930s and reduced growth rates thereafter, recurrent fears of an energy crisis, the depletion of resources and concurrent global pollution, famine and genocidal dictators in parts of Africa and Asia, the rise of an aggressive religious fundamentalism in the Muslim world, and widespread political terrorism in the Middle East and Europe. The superpowers never ceased to compete in the realms of strategic weapons and influence in the Third World and thus failed to sustain their brief experiment with détente. As President Jimmy Carter's national security adviser, Zbigniew Brzezinski, concluded: "The factors that make for international instability are gaining the historical upper hand over the forces that work for more organized cooperation. The unavoidable conclusion of any detached analysis of global trends is that social turmoil, political unrest, economic crisis, and international friction are likely to become more widespread during the remainder of this century."

The Decline of Détente

General Secretary Brezhnev and President Nixon were understandably optimistic in the wake of the endorsement by the 24th Party Congress of the Soviet peace program in 1971 and Nixon's landslide reelection in 1972. Both expected their new relationship to mature over the course of Nixon's second term. Détente, however, had fragile foundations in foreign as well as domestic policy. The Soviets viewed it as a form of mere peaceful coexistence in which revolutionary forces could be expected to take advantage of the new American restraint, while the U.S. administration implicitly sold détente as a means of restraining Communist activity around the world. American conservatives were bound to lose faith in détente with each new incident of Soviet assertiveness, while liberals remained hostile to Nixon himself, his realpolitik, and his predilection for the use of force. Between 1973 and 1976 Soviet advances in the Third World, the destruction of Nixon's presidency in the Watergate scandal, and congressional actions to limit the foreign policy prerogatives of the White House undermined the domestic foundations of détente. After 1977 the U.S.S.R. seemed to take advantage of the Carter administration's vacillations in Third World conflicts and in arms-control talks, until the Democrats themselves reluctantly announced the demise of détente following the Soviet invasion of Afghanistan in 1979.

LIMITATIONS ON EXECUTIVE POWER

Analysts with a sufficiently historical point of view tended to see in the Watergate affair and Nixon's 1974 resignation the culmination of a 30-year trend by which war and the Cold War had greatly expanded, and ultimately corrupted, executive power. Liberals who, in Eisenhower's time, had called for strong presidential leadership now bemoaned "the imperial presidency." With what were widely understood to be the lessons of Vietnam fresh in the nation's mind, and a majority in Congress and the press hostile to the sitting president, the moment arrived for a legislative counterattack on the executive. This interpretation is borne out by the subsequent congressional acts designed to limit executive freedom in foreign policy.

The War Powers Act of 1973 restrained the president's ability to commit U.S. forces overseas. The Stevenson and Jackson–Vanik amendments imposed conditions (regarding Soviet policy on Jewish emigration) on administration plans to expand trade with the U.S.S.R. In 1974–75 Congress prevented the president from involving the United States in a crisis in Cyprus or aiding anti-Communist forces in Angola and passed the Arms Export Control Act, removing presidential discretion in supplying arms overseas. New financial controls limited the president's ability to conclude executive agreements with foreign powers, of which some 6,300 had been signed between 1946 and 1974 as compared with only 411 treaties requiring the Senate's advice and consent. Finally, revelations of past CIA covert operations, including schemes to assassinate Fidel Castro, inspired complicated congressional oversight procedures for U.S. intelligence agencies. These assaults on executive prerogative were meant to prevent future Vietnams, prevent unelected presidential aides from engaging in secret diplomacy, and restore to Congress an "appropriate" role in foreign policy. Critics of the limitations held that no great power could conduct a coherent or effective foreign policy under such a combination of openness and restrictions, especially in a world populated increasingly by totalitarian regimes, guerrilla movements, and terrorists.

SECURITY TALKS

The Nixon–Brezhnev summits of 1973–74 produced only minor follow-ons in the area of arms control—the uncontroversial Agreement on the Prevention of Nuclear War and an agreement to reduce the number of ABM sites from the two permitted in 1972 to one. Gerald Ford, president from August 1974, and Henry Kissinger, who remained as secretary of state, attempted to restore the momentum of détente through a new SALT agreement regulating the dangerous race in MIRVed missiles, which SALT I had not prevented. The United States proposed strict equality in nuclear delivery systems and total throw weight, which meant that the United States would be allowed to MIRV more of its missiles to offset the greater size of Soviet missiles. Since the United States had no plans for a unilateral buildup in any case, however, the Soviets had no incentive to make such a concession. Instead, Ford and Brezhnev signed an Interim Agreement at Vladivostok in November 1974 that limited each side to 2,400 delivery vehicles, of which 1,320 could be MIRVed. While the Soviets claimed that this was a concession, since they declined to count the 90 British and French missiles aimed at them, the Soviets' giant SS-18s, able to deliver up to 10 MIRVs, ensured the U.S.S.R. an advantage in ICBM warheads. The repeated failure to restrain the growth of Soviet offensive systems soon sparked fears that the United States might become vulnerable to preemptive attack.

Meanwhile, the mid-1970s brought to a logical conclusion the process of détente in Europe. Nixon and Kissinger, aware that the United States had seemed to ignore its European allies during the 10 years of Vietnam, declared 1973 "the year of Europe" and hoped to forestall NATO governments from bargaining with Moscow on their own. Watergate and the Arab–Israeli war of that year (the Yom Kippur War) turned this initiative into a public-relations failure, however. Instead, the United States was obliged to follow the European lead in the ongoing Conference on Security and Cooperation in Europe and negotiations toward a "mutual and balanced force reduction" treaty covering NATO and Warsaw Pact forces in central Europe.

The climax of the security talks was the Helsinki summit of 35 nations in the summer of 1975 and an agglomeration of proposals divided into three "baskets." (A fourth basket dealt with the question of a follow-up conference.) In Basket I the signatories accepted the inviolability of Europe's existing borders and the principle of noninterference in the internal affairs of other states—thereby recognizing formally the Soviet gains in World War II and the Soviet-bloc states. Basket II promoted exchanges in science, technology, and commerce, expanding Soviet access to Western technology and opening the Soviet market to western European industry. Basket III, the apparent Soviet concession, aimed at expanding cultural and humanitarian cooperation among all states on the basis of respect for human rights. Not surprisingly, Western opinion of the Helsinki Accords, and of détente in general, came to rest heavily on whether the U.S.S.R. would voluntarily comply with Basket III. American leaders of both parties considered Helsinki misguided and empty, especially after Moscow stepped up the persecution of dissidents and jailed those of their citizens engaged in a "Helsinki watch" on Soviet compliance. In sum, Helsinki (and U.S. demands on behalf of Soviet Jews) pointed up another contradiction in détente, this time between American insistence on Soviet liberalization and Soviet insistence on noninterference in the domestic politics of other states.

EVENTS IN SOUTHEAST ASIA AND AFRICA

During final negotiations at Helsinki, events in Southeast Asia compounded the American sense of humiliation and growing discontent with détente. The North Vietnamese had never viewed the 1973 peace accords as anything other than an interlude permitting the final withdrawal of American forces. In the year following they built up their strength in South Vietnam to more than 150,000 regulars armed with Soviet tanks, artillery, and antiaircraft weapons. The ARVN was poorly trained, suffered from low morale after the Americans were gone, and faced an enemy able to attack at times and places of its own choosing. The American withdrawal also removed at a blow some 300,000 jobs from the local economy, and President Thieu made matters worse by trying to establish one-party bureaucratic rule without the charisma or prestige to sustain it.

By October 1974 the Politburo in Hanoi concluded that the Saigon regime was ripe for collapse. Large-scale probes of ARVN defenses in January 1975 confirmed their optimism. By the end of the month 12 provinces and 8,000,000 people had fallen to the Communists. On April 10, unable to obtain congressional approval of $422,000,000 in further military aid, President Ford declared that the Vietnam War was over "as far as America is concerned." The final North Vietnamese offensive reached Saigon on April 30, 1975, as the last remaining Americans fled to helicopters atop the U.S. embassy. Hanoi triumphantly reunified Vietnam politically in July 1976 and confined thousands of South Vietnamese to "reeducation camps," while thousands of "boat people" risked death in the South China Sea to escape reprisals and Communism.

The end in Cambodia had already occurred. The Communist Khmer Rouge cut off the capital, Phnom Penh, in January 1975.

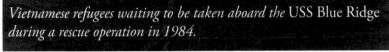

Vietnamese refugees waiting to be taken aboard the USS Blue Ridge during a rescue operation in 1984.

When the U.S. Congress denied further aid to Cambodia, Lon Nol fled, and in mid-April the Khmer Rouge took control. Its leader, Pol Pot, was a French-educated disciple of Maoist "total revolution" to whom everything traditional was anathema. The Khmer Rouge reign of terror became one of the worst holocausts of the 20th century. All urban dwellers, including hospital patients, were forced into the countryside in order to build a new society of rural communes. Sexual intercourse was forbidden and the family abolished. More than 100,000 Cambodians, including all "bourgeois," or educated people, were killed outright, and 400,000 succumbed in the death marches; in all, 1,200,000 people (a fifth of the Cambodian nation) perished. The Khmer Rouge, however, were not allied with Hanoi, and in 1979 PAVN forces invaded Cambodia to oust the Khmer Rouge and install a puppet regime. This action completed the conquest of Indochina by North Vietnam, for Laos, too, became Communist after the fall of Saigon. Thus the domino theory was at last put to the test and to a large extent borne out.

Events in Africa as well seemed to bear out the Soviet expectation that "progressive forces" would gain ground rapidly during the new era of superpower parity. Angola and Mozambique, coastal states facing the oil-tanker routes around the Cape of Good Hope, were finally slated to achieve independence from Portugal following a leftist military coup in Lisbon in April 1974. Three indigenous groups, each linked to tribal factions, vied for predominance in Angola. The MPLA (Popular Movement for the Liberation of Angola) of Agostinho Neto was Marxist and received aid from the U.S.S.R. and Cuba. The FNLA (National Front for the Liberation of Angola) in the north was backed by Mobutu Sese Seko of Zaire (now the Democratic Republic of the Congo) and initially by a token contribution from the CIA. In the south the UNITA (National

THE KHMER ROUGE

Khmer Rouge was a radical communist movement that ruled Cambodia from 1975 to 1979 after winning power through a guerrilla war. It was purportedly set up in 1967 as the armed wing of the Communist Party of Kampuchea.

Cambodia's communist movement originated in the Khmer People's Revolutionary Party, which was formed in 1951 under the auspices of the Viet Minh of Vietnam. The party's largely French-educated Marxist leaders eventually renamed it the Communist Party of Kampuchea. By the late 1950s the party's members were engaged in clandestine activities against the government of Prince Norodom Sihanouk, but for many years they made little headway against Sihanouk from their bases in remote jungle and mountain areas, partly because of Sihanouk's own popularity among the peasants whom the communists sought to incite to rebellion.

After a right-wing military coup toppled Sihanouk in 1970, however, the Khmer Rouge entered into a political coalition with him and began attracting increased support in the Cambodian countryside, a trend that was accelerated by the destructive U.S. bombing campaigns over Cambodia in the early 1970s. By this time the Khmer Rouge were also receiving substantial aid from North Vietnam, which had withheld its support during the years of Sihanouk's rule.

In a civil war that continued for nearly five years from 1970, the Khmer Rouge gradually expanded the areas of the Cambodian countryside under their control. Finally, in April 1975, Khmer Rouge forces mounted a victorious attack on the capital city of Phnom Penh and established a national government to rule Cambodia. The military leader of the Khmer Rouge, Pol Pot, became the new government's prime minister. The Khmer Rouge's rule over the next four years was marked by some of the worst excesses of any Marxist government in the 20th century, during which an estimated 1.5 million (and possibly up to 2 million) Cambodians died and many of the country's professional and technical class were exterminated.

The Khmer Rouge government was overthrown in 1979 by invading Vietnamese troops, who installed a puppet government propped up by Vietnamese aid and expertise. The Khmer Rouge retreated to remote areas and resumed guerrilla warfare, this time operating from bases near the border with Thailand and obtaining aid from China. The Khmer Rouge opposed the United Nations–sponsored peace settlement of 1991 and the multiparty elections in 1993, and they continued guerrilla warfare against the noncommunist coalition government formed after those elections. The disarray within the organization intensified in 1997, when Pol Pot was arrested by other Khmer Rouge leaders and sentenced to life imprisonment. Pol Pot died in 1998, and soon afterward the surviving leaders of the Khmer Rouge defected or were imprisoned.

Talks aimed at bringing the Khmer Rouge's surviving leaders to trial began almost immediately after the movement's demise. After years of wrangling and delay, the Extraordinary Chambers in the Courts of Cambodia (commonly called the Khmer Rouge Tribunal) was established in 2006 as a joint operation between the United Nations and the government of Cambodia. The first indictments were handed down in 2007, and the first trial—against Kaing Guek Eav (better known as Duch), the former commander of a notorious Khmer Rouge prison—got under way in 2009. In 2010 Duch was convicted of war crimes and of crimes against humanity and was sentenced to prison.

Union for the Total Independence of Angola) of Jonas Savimbi had ties to China but came to rely increasingly on white South Africa. In the Alvor agreement of January 1975 all three agreed to form a coalition, but civil war resumed in July.

By the end of the year the MPLA had been reinforced by 10,000 Cuban soldiers airlifted to Luanda by the U.S.S.R. In the United States the imperative of "no more Vietnams" and congressional ire over CIA covert operations frustrated Ford's desire to help non-Communist Angolans. Neto accordingly proclaimed a People's Republic of Angola in November 1975 and signed a Treaty of Friendship with the U.S.S.R. the following October. The rebel factions, however, remained in control of much of the country, and Cuban troop levels eventually reached 19,000. A Marxist government also assumed power in Mozambique.

AMERICAN UNCERTAINTY

In winning the presidential election of 1976, Jimmy Carter capitalized on the American people's disgust with Vietnam and Watergate by promising little more than an open and honest administration. Though intelligent and earnest, he lacked the experience and acumen necessary to provide strong leadership in foreign policy. This deficiency was especially unfortunate since his major advisers had sharply divergent views on the proper American posture toward the Soviet Union.

Carter's inaugural address showed how much he diverged from the realpolitik of Nixon and Kissinger. Such a sentiment as "Because we are free we can never be indifferent to the fate of freedom elsewhere" recalled Kennedy's 1961 call to arms. But Carter made clear that his emphasis on human rights applied at least as much to authoritarian governments friendly to the United States as to Communist states, and that such idealism was in fact, as he put it on another occasion, the most "practical and realistic approach" to foreign policy. He hoped to divert American energies away from preoccupation with relations with the U.S.S.R. toward global problems such as energy, population control, hunger, curbing of arms sales, and nuclear proliferation. Carter's first initiative in the perilous field of arms control was an embarrassing failure. Rejecting his own secretary of state's advice to take a gradual approach, he startled the Soviets with a deep-cut proposal for immediate elimination of as much as 25 percent of the U.S. and Soviet strategic missiles and a freeze on new long-range missile deployment. Brezhnev rejected it out of hand, and Foreign Minister Andrey Gromyko called this attempt to scrap the Vladivostok formula a "cheap and shady maneuver."

Carter was to gain one stunning success during his term, a peace treaty between Egypt and Israel, but he was unable to stem the growth of Soviet influence in Africa. Somalia, on the strategic Horn of Africa astride the Red Sea and Indian Ocean shipping lanes, had been friendly to Moscow since 1969. In September 1974 a pro-Marxist military junta overthrew the government of neighbouring Ethiopia, had Emperor Haile Selassie confined in his palace (where he was later suffocated in his bed), and invited Soviet and Cuban advisers into the country. The Somalis then took advantage of the turmoil—perversely, from Moscow's point of view—to reassert old claims to the Ogaden region of Ethiopia and to invade, while Eritrean rebels also took up arms against Addis Ababa. The Soviets and Cubans stepped up support for Ethiopia, while Castro vainly urged all parties to form a "Marxist federation."

Carter at first cut off aid to Ethiopia on the ground of human-rights abuses and promised weapons for the Somalis. By August he realized that the arms would only be used in the Ogaden campaign and reversed himself, making the United States appear ignorant and indecisive. Somalia broke with the U.S.S.R. anyway, but 17,000 Cuban troops and $1,000,000,000 in Soviet aid allowed Ethiopia to clear the Ogaden of invaders and in 1978 to suppress the Eritrean revolt. Ethiopia signed its own treaty of friendship and cooperation with the U.S.S.R. in November. The failure of the Carter administration either to consult with the Soviets or to resist Soviet–Cuban military intervention set a bad precedent and weakened both détente and U.S. prestige in the Third World.

The events in the Horn of Africa, which Brzezinski interpreted as part of a Soviet strategy to outflank the oil-rich Persian Gulf so vital to Western economies, encouraged the United States to seek help in balancing Soviet power in the world. The obvious means of doing so was to complete the rapprochement with China begun under Nixon. Some advisers opposed "playing the China card" for fear that the Soviets would retaliate by calling off the continuing SALT negotiations, but Brzezinski persuaded the president that closer ties between the United States and China would oblige the U.S.S.R. to court the United States, as had occurred in 1972.

Brzezinski went to Peking in May 1978 to initiate discussions leading toward full diplomatic recognition. His cause was aided by important changes in the Chinese leadership. Zhou Enlai and Mao Zedong had died in 1976. Hua Guofeng won the initial power struggle and ordered the arrest and trial of the radical Gang of Four led by Mao's wife, Jiang Qing. Both superpowers hoped that the suppression of radicals in favour of pragmatists in the Chinese government might portend better relations with Peking. The rehabilitation of the formerly condemned "capitalist roader" Deng Xiaoping led to a resumption of Soviet–Chinese border clashes, however, and the clear shift of Vietnam into the Soviet camp strengthened Washington's hand in Peking. Hua and Carter announced in December 1978 that full diplomatic relations would be established on January 1, 1979. The United States downgraded its representation in Taiwan and renounced its 1954 mutual defense treaty with the Nationalist Chinese.

The spectre of a possible Sino-American alliance may have alarmed the Soviets (Brezhnev warned Carter not to sell arms to China) but was never a real possibility. The Chinese remained

Communist and distrustful of the United States. They made clear that China was no card to be played at will by one or the other of the superpowers. Nor could China's underdeveloped economy sustain a large conventional war or the projection of force overseas (which the United States would not want in any case), while in nuclear systems China was as weak vis-à-vis the Soviet Union as the Soviet Union had been vis-à-vis the United States in the 1950s. Ties to the United States might provide China with high technology, but the United States was no more willing to place nuclear or missile systems in Chinese hands than Khrushchev had been. To be sure, the United States had an interest in preventing a Sino-Soviet rapprochement (an estimated 11 percent of the Soviet military effort was devoted to the Chinese front), but any pause given the U.S.S.R. by Sino-American cooperation was probably more useful to China than to the United States. Indeed, Peking was quite capable of playing its U.S. card to carry out adventures of its own.

THE SINO-VIETNAMESE WAR AND SALT II

After their 1975 victory the North Vietnamese showed a natural strategic preference for the distant U.S.S.R. and fell out with their historic enemy, neighbouring China. In quick succession Vietnam expelled Chinese merchants, opened Cam Ranh Bay to the Soviet navy, and signed a treaty of friendship with Moscow. Vietnamese troops had also invaded Cambodia to oust the pro-Peking Khmer Rouge. Soon after Deng Xiaoping's celebrated visit to the United States, Peking announced its intention to punish the Vietnamese, and, in February 1979, its forces invaded Vietnam in strength. The Carter administration felt obliged to favour China (especially given residual American hostility to North Vietnam) and supported Peking's offer to evacuate Vietnam only when Vietnam evacuated Cambodia. The Soviets reacted with threats against China, but Chinese forces performed abysmally even against Vietnam's frontier militia, and after three weeks of hard fighting, in which Vietnam claimed to have inflicted 45,000 casualties, the Chinese withdrew. The results for U.S. policy were all negative: Chinese military prestige was shattered, Cambodia remained in the Soviet-Vietnamese camp, and the tactic of playing the China card was rendered ridiculous.

To the chagrin of Peking, the Sino-Vietnamese War failed to forestall a planned U.S.–Soviet summit meeting and the signing of a second arms agreement, SALT II. After Carter's first deep-cut proposal, negotiations had resumed on the basis of the Vladivostok agreement and had finally produced a draft treaty. The summit was held in Vienna in June 1979, and Carter returned to seek congressional approval for SALT II as well as most-favoured-nation trade status for both the U.S.S.R. and China. The treaty inspired widespread suspicion in the U.S. Senate on its own merits. The modest limits on nuclear forces and allowances for upgrading existing missiles did not seem sufficient to prevent the Soviets' superior long-range missile forces from threatening the survival of U.S. land-based missiles. The American will to upgrade its own deterrent, meanwhile, seemed to be sapped by the SALT process itself. Confusion reigned over how the MX missile might be deployed so as to survive a Soviet first strike, and Carter cancelled programs to deploy the B-1 strategic bomber and an antitank neutron bomb designed for Europe. There also was widespread doubt over whether Soviet compliance with SALT II could be adequately monitored. The treaty foundered as well on growing American impatience with Communist expansion in the Third World.

Any chance of Senate ratification of SALT II disappeared on December 25, 1979, when the U.S.S.R. launched an invasion of

Afghanistan to prop up a friendly regime. Even after a decade of détente the American public still thought viscerally in terms of containment, and this latest and most brazen Soviet advance pushed the president over the fence. "This action of the Soviets," said Carter, "has made a more dramatic change in my own opinion of what the Soviets' ultimate goals are than anything they've done." Calling the Afghan invasion "a clear threat to peace," Carter ordered an embargo on sales of grain and high-technology equipment to the U.S.S.R., canceled U.S. participation in the 1980 Moscow Olympic Games, reinstated registration for the draft, withdrew the SALT II treaty from the Senate, and proclaimed the Carter Doctrine, pledging the United States to the defense of the Persian Gulf. It was clear to all that détente was dead. Both the United States and the Soviet Union voluntarily observed the arms limits agreed upon in SALT II in subsequent years, however.

Many nations boycotted the 1980 Moscow Olympic Games in protest of the Soviet Union's invasion of Afghanistan.

POSTMORTEM

Was détente a failure because the Soviets refused to play by the rules, because the United States was unwilling to accord the U.S.S.R. genuine equality, or because détente was never really tried at all? Or did the differing U.S. and Soviet conceptions of détente ensure that, sooner or later, American patience would wear thin? The last explanation is, in foreshortened perspective, at least, the most convincing.

From the Soviet point of view the United States had been a hegemonic power from 1945 to 1972, secure in its nuclear dominance and free to undertake military and political intervention around the world. The correlation of forces had gradually shifted, however, to the point where the U.S.S.R. could rightly claim global equality and respect for "peaceful coexistence." Under détente, therefore, the United States was obliged to recognize Soviet interests in all regions of the world and to understand that the U.S.S.R. was now as free as the United States to defend those interests with diplomacy and arms. Those interests included, above all, fraternal aid for "progressive" movements in the Third World. Détente certainly could never mean the freezing of the status quo or the trends of history as understood in Marxist theory. Instead, in the Soviet view, the United States continued to resent Soviet equality in armaments, to shut the U.S.S.R. out of regional diplomacy (as in the Middle East), to interfere in Soviet domestic policy, to support counterrevolutionary movements, and, in violation of the spirit of détente, to attempt to organize the encirclement of the U.S.S.R. in league with NATO and China.

From the American perspective, Soviet policy from 1945 to 1972 was characterized by a Marxist-Leninist drive to export revolution and achieve world dominion by dividing and bullying the West and exploiting the struggles of Third World nations. At the same time the growing maturity of the U.S.S.R. itself, the split in world Communism, and the realization that the Western world was not about to collapse (from either "the contradictions of capitalism" or Soviet subversion) had made Cold War obsolete. Under détente, therefore, the U.S.S.R. was obliged to accept the responsibilities as well as the benefits of membership in the comity of civilized states, to reduce its exorbitant military spending and subversive activity, and to cease trying to turn the domestic problems of other countries to unilateral benefit. Instead, in the American view, the U.S.S.R. continued to exploit Western restraint, to build up its nuclear and conventional forces far beyond the needs of deterrence, and to exploit Communist proxy forces to take over developing nations.

Each view had a basis in reality, and, given the differing assumptions of the two governments, each was persuasive. The burden of compromise or dissolution of the relationship fell inevitably on the democratic, status quo power, however, and in time American opinion would cease to tolerate Soviet advances made under the guise of détente. The notion of détente was flawed from the start in two crucial points. First, with the exception of preventing nuclear war, the United States and the U.S.S.R. still shared no major interests in the world; and second, the specific agreements on respect for spheres of influence included Europe and isolated regions elsewhere but not the bulk of the Third World. Americans inevitably viewed any Soviet assertiveness in such undefined regions as evidence of the same old Soviet drive for world domination, while the Soviets inevitably viewed any American protestations as evidence of the same old American strategy of containment. Within a decade, the hopes raised by Nixon and Brezhnev stood exposed as illusory.

The Arab-Israeli Conflict

Among the manifestations of the diffusion of political power in the world after 1957 was the rise of regional powers and conflicts with only distant or secondary connections to the rivalries of the Cold War blocs, of multilateral political and economic pressure groups, and of revolutionary, terrorist, or religious movements operating across national boundaries ("nonstate actors"). The politics of the Middle East after 1972 comprised all three and so frustrated attempts by the industrial states to control events in the region that by 1978 Brzezinski was describing the old southern tier of states reaching beneath the U.S.S.R. from Egypt to Pakistan as the "arc of crisis."

The sweeping Israeli victory in the Six-Day War of 1967 had forced every Arab state to rethink its own foreign policy and the extent of its commitment to the cause of Arab unity. Egypt, having lost the Sinai, faced Israelis entrenched in the Bar-Lev line directly across the Suez Canal. Jordan, having lost the West Bank, faced Israeli troops directly across the Jordan River. Syria, having lost the Golan Heights, faced Israeli forces within easy striking distance of Damascus itself. The notion of united Arab armies sweeping the Jews into the sea had clearly proved to be romantic. Political unity among the Arabs suffered from the abiding division between nationalist and socialist states like Egypt, Syria, and Iraq and traditional Arab monarchies like Saudi Arabia and Jordan.

PALESTINIAN TERRORISM

The Palestine Liberation Organization (PLO) was organized in 1964 to represent some 2,000,000 refugees from the Palestine mandate who were scattered around the Arab world. From 1968 led by Yāsir ʿArafāt, the PLO was also divided between old families of notables, whose authority dated back to Ottoman times, and young middle-class or fedayeen factions anxious to exert pressure on Israel and the West through terrorism. The latter included the Popular Front for the Liberation of Palestine (PFLP), formed three months after the 1967 war. Over the next year the PFLP hijacked 14 foreign airliners, culminating in its spectacular destruction of four planes at once in Jordan.

In 1970–71 the moderate King Hussein of Jordan lost patience with the autonomous PLO formations in his territory and expelled them, provoking a sharp military exchange with Syria. The PLO moved its central offices to Lebanon, whence terrorists could cross the frontier to commit atrocities against civilians inside Israel. The PFLP and other Palestinian groups also linked up with extreme conspiracies in Italy, Austria, and Germany to form a terrorist network that left no European or Mediterranean state free from the fear of random violence. In September 1972 terrorists from an organization calling itself Black September took nine Israeli athletes hostage at the Munich Olympic Games; all the hostages and five terrorists died in the ensuing gun battle with police.

The terrorist network benefited mightily from the financial support, training, or refuge provided by established pro-Soviet states like Cuba, East Germany, Bulgaria, Algeria, Syria, Yemen (Aden), and especially Libya. In 1969 the Libyan monarchy was overthrown in a military coup led by Colonel Muammar al-Qaddafi, a fanatical adherent of Nasser's pan-Arabism. Following Nasser's death in 1970 and the development of rich oil deposits in Libya, Qaddafi styled himself as the new leader and financier of the radical Arab cause. In imitation of Mao, he issued a little *Green Book* describing his "new gospel.... One of its words can destroy the world." The ideology was a mixture of Third World-ism, Socialism, and Muslim fundamentalism, and it called forth a "heroic politics." In the eyes of the West, the rhetoric masked a crazed cruelty, and even in Arab eyes it seemed at best antiquated in the wake of the 1967 war.

Another new feature of Middle Eastern politics was the assertiveness of the Organization of Petroleum Exporting Countries (OPEC), composed of oil-producing countries in the Persian Gulf and Arabian Peninsula as well as Libya, Nigeria, and Venezuela. The members of this producers' cartel accounted for a large percentage of the world's oil reserves and wielded tremendous potential power over the Europeans and Japanese, who relied on imports for more than 80 percent of their energy needs. In the past, oil prices had been kept artificially low by the Western oil companies through bilateral agreements with producer states. By 1970, however, most host governments had taken over ownership of the production facilities, and they saw in a drastic rise of oil prices a means of accumulating capital for development and purchases of arms, as well as a way to pressure the Western states into respecting their grievances against Israel.

Egypt was the most populous frontline (*i.e.*, bordering Israel) Arab state, but it did not have oil revenues. Since 1955 Egypt had undergone a demographic explosion. Population was growing at a rate of 1,000,000 per year, and 35,000,000 people were crowded into the Nile valley and delta. The numbers and youth of the Egyptians (over half were under 25 in 1980) and the country's economic weakness meant that frustrated and unemployed youth posed the constant threat of political instability. Certainly Egypt could no longer afford an endless crusade against Israel. These considerations dominated the thinking of Nasser's successor as president, Anwar el-Sādāt. He could not, however, abandon Nasser's legacy, especially with the Sinai under Israeli occupation, without losing his legitimacy at home. Accordingly, Sādāt laid a risky and courageous plan to extricate his country from its foreign and domestic stalemates. Husbanding the arms provided by the U.S.S.R. after 1967, he abruptly expelled 20,000 Soviet advisers in July 1972 and opened a secret channel to Washington, hinting that Egypt and the United States together could eliminate Soviet involvement in the Middle East. Only the Americans, he reasoned, might influence the Israelis to return the occupied regions. Then, on Oct. 6, 1973, during the Jewish holiday of Yom Kippur, he launched the fourth Arab–Israeli war.

THE YOM KIPPUR WAR

The Egyptian army moved across the Suez Canal in force and engaged the Bar-Lev line. For the first time it made substantial progress and inflicted a level of casualties especially damaging for the outnumbered Israelis. Syrian forces also stormed the Golan Heights. The intensity of the Egyptian and Syrian assault, so unlike the situation in 1967, rapidly began to exhaust Israel's reserve stocks of munitions. The United States and the Soviet Union reacted with subtle attempts to fine-tune the outcome by alternately withholding or providing arms to the belligerents and by urging or discouraging a UN cease-fire. Nixon denied Israel an airlift of arms until October 13, preventing Israel from launching a prompt counterattack and thereby signaling Sādāt of American sympathy. The reluctance of the United States to help Israel changed rapidly when the Soviet Union commenced its own resupply effort to Egypt and Syria. Once assured of U.S. aid, however, the Israelis struck on both fronts. Israel succeeded in disabling portions of the Egyptian air defenses, which allowed Israeli forces commanded by Gen. Ariel Sharon to cross the Suez Canal and surround the Egyptian Third Army. On the Golan front, Israeli troops, at heavy cost, repulsed the Syrians and advanced to the edge of the Golan plateau on the road to Damascus.

Kissinger, alarmed that the Israeli victory might be so complete as to hinder a lasting settlement, quickly agreed to call, with the Soviet Union, for a UN cease-fire. The cease-fire broke down at once, and Israeli forces encircled a 20,000-man Egyptian army corps. Brezhnev curtly warned Nixon of possible Soviet military intervention, which the United States moved to deter, perhaps recklessly, with a worldwide alert of its military forces. Finally, Kissinger threatened a cutoff of arms deliveries unless Israel halted its offensive, and peace was restored.

The 1973 war, known as both the Yom Kippur War and the Ramadan War because it took place during both of those religious holidays, saved Egyptian honour and solidified Sādāt's prestige to the point where he could afford to be conciliatory. The United States emerged as the "honest broker" between Egypt and Israel. As Kissinger put it, "The Arabs can get guns from the Russians, but they can get their territory back only from us." Kissinger's "shuttle diplomacy" between Tel Aviv and Cairo secured an Israeli withdrawal beyond the Suez in January 1974, the reopening of the canal, the insertion of a UN force between the antagonists, and, in September 1975, an Israeli retreat from the crucial Mitla and Gidi passes in the Sinai. The United States flooded both countries with economic and military aid, and Sādāt repudiated Nasser's Socialism in favour of policies stimulating domestic private enterprise. On May 31, 1974, Israel and Syria signed a cease-fire agreement that also covered separation of their forces by a UN buffer zone and exchange of prisoners of war. In June the oil embargo was lifted.

The limited rapprochement that emerged from the 1973 war was purchased at great economic cost, for the Arab OPEC nations, led by Saudi Arabia, seized the opportunity to enact a five-month embargo of oil exports to all nations aiding Israel.

More telling still was the price revolution that preceded and followed. OPEC had already engineered a doubling of the posted price of oil to $3.07 per barrel by the eve of the war. In January 1974 it nearly quadrupled the price again, to $11.56 per barrel. The importance of this sudden rise cannot be exaggerated. The resulting shortages and exorbitant costs accelerated the growing inflation in the Western world, exposed the energy-dependency of the industrial nations, created a vast balance-of-payments deficit in many industrial states, wiped out the hard-won economic progress of many developing nations, and placed massive sums of petrodollars in the hands of a few underpopulated Middle Eastern states. The political upshot was that the United States and Europe would have to pay close attention to the desires of those Arab states in foreign policy as long as OPEC unity survived.

THE CAMP DAVID ACCORDS

In November 1977, Sādāt shocked the Arab world by announcing his willingness to go to Jerusalem personally to seek peace. When his talks with the new Israeli prime minister, Menachem Begin, broke down, President Carter invited them both to Camp David in September 1978. During 13 days of intensive discussion, Carter succeeded in bringing the rivals together.

It was extremely unusual for heads of state to engage in a summit meeting at which the outcome was so much in doubt. Not only had Egypt and Israel been at war for decades, but the personality differences of the leaders promised to complicate the dialogue. Begin was pessimistic about what he believed could be achieved at Camp David and insisted that the objective be limited to developing an agenda for future meetings. By contrast, Sādāt was willing to join in comprehensive negotiations aimed at settling all controversial issues during the few

From left, Anwar el-Sādāt, Jimmy Carter, and Menachem Begin during the Camp David negotiations in September 1978.

days of the summit. Carter insisted that there be no direct press coverage of the meetings, fearing it would have a negative effect on negotiations.

After three days of negotiations, the heated discussions reached an impasse, and direct discourse between Sādāt and Begin became impossible. Carter then compiled a single document that encompassed a resolution of the major issues, presented the proposals to each leader in separate meetings, assessed their comments, and redrafted the manuscript some two dozen times, shuttling the manuscript back and forth for their review. As the days passed, prospects for a settlement at Camp David appeared so bleak that Sādāt threatened to leave, and Carter began planning to return to the White House and suffer the likely political consequences of failure. An agreement was reached on the final day, however, when, at the last minute, Begin agreed to allow the Knesset to decide the fate of the settlements Israelis had established on the Sinai Peninsula (which Sādāt had required dismantled and Begin had sworn not to abandon).

The Camp David Accords provided for complete Israeli evacuation of the Sinai, gradual progress toward self-rule for West Bank Palestinians over a five-year period, and a peace treaty signed by Begin and Sādāt at the White House in March 1979. Sādāt and Begin were awarded the Nobel Prize for Peace in 1978 for their contributions to the agreements. However, this historic settlement dismayed other Arab states and split the PLO asunder, the so-called rejectionists refusing to recognize the settlement. Qaddafi purchased huge amounts of Soviet arms and expanded Libya's training and supply of terrorists. In December 1979, 300 Muslim fundamentalists seized the holiest of all Islāmic shrines in Mecca. Egypt was expelled from the Arab League, and Sādāt himself was assassinated by Arab extremists in 1981, during the Armed Forces Day military parade commemorating the Yom Kippur War.

The Iranian Revolution and Hostage Crisis

Carter's success in Middle Eastern diplomacy was likewise undercut by the collapse of the strongest and staunchest American ally in the Muslim world, the Shah of Iran. Since the monarchy had been restored by a CIA-aided coup in 1953, Reza Shah Pahlavi had used Iran's oil revenues to finance rapid modernization of his country and the purchase of American arms. Nixon had chosen Iran to be a U.S. surrogate in the vital Persian Gulf, and as late as 1977 Carter praised the Shah for making Iran "an island of stability." Clearly, American intelligence services failed to detect the widespread Iranian resentment of modernization (meaning, in this context, materialism, emancipation of women, and secularization), middle-class opposition to the autocracy, and the rising tide of Shī'ite fundamentalism that were undermining the Shah's legitimacy. Fundamentalist movements and conflicts between Sunnite and Shī'ite Muslims have arisen periodically in the course of Islāmic history, but the outbreaks of the late 20th century were especially notable in light of the Western assumption that less developed countries would naturally secularize their politics and culture as they modernized their society and economy. Instead, rapidly developing Iran succumbed to a religious revolution led by Ayatollah Ruhollah Khomeini.

By November 1978 the beleaguered Shah saw his options reduced to democratization, military repression, or abdication. Despite the importance of Iran for U.S. interests, including the presence there of critical electronic listening posts used to monitor missile tests inside the U.S.S.R., Carter was unable to choose between personal loyalty toward an old ally and the moral argument on behalf of reform or abdication. In January 1979 the Shah left Iran; the next month, when he requested asylum in the United States, Carter refused lest he give offense to the new Iranian regime. The gesture did not help the United States, however. An interim government in Tehrān quickly gave way to a theocracy under Khomeini, who arrived in Iran amid wild rejoicing on February 1 and declared Iran an Islamic republic on April 1. Elements within the clergy promptly moved to exclude their former left-wing, nationalist, and intellectual allies from any positions of power in the new regime, and a return to conservative social values was enforced. The violence and brutality often exceeded that which had taken place under the Shah. The militias and the clerics they supported made every effort to suppress Western cultural influence, and, facing persecution and violence, many of the Western-educated elite fled the country.

Khomeini, who denounced the United States as a "great Satan," approved the seizure on November 4, 1979, of the American embassy in Tehrān and the holding of 63 hostages there. It soon became evident that no one within the virulently anti-American atmosphere of postrevolutionary Iran was willing, or able, to release the hostages. The hostage takers themselves most likely were supporters of Khomeini; he demanded, as a condition of the hostages' release, the extradition of the Shah, who at that time was undergoing medical treatment in the United States. Khomeini did, however, order the release of 13 hostages on November 17; another, who became gravely ill, was released on July 11, 1980, producing the final number of 52 hostages.

Ayatollah Ruhollah Khomeini returns to Iran on February 1, 1979, after fifteen years of exile.

The hostage situation dragged on for nearly 15 months, and most Americans were infuriated by the unfathomable Khomeini and frustrated by Carter's apparent ineffectiveness. U.S. diplomats twice obtained United Nations (UN) Security Council resolutions (on December 4 and 31) against Iran's actions. Carter reacted to the crisis by adopting Brzezinski's formula that the Middle East and South Asia constituted an arc of crisis susceptible to Soviet adventurism. In his State of the Union address of January 1980 he enunciated the Carter Doctrine, declaring that any attempt by an outside force

One of the American hostages (center), *who were held at the American embassy in Tehrān for over fourteen months.*

to gain control of the Persian Gulf would be viewed as an attack on the vital interests of the United States, and he pledged to form a Rapid Deployment Force to defend the region. Whether the U.S. military was truly capable of sustained combat in that remote region was doubtful.

When diplomacy failed to free the hostages in Tehrān, Carter resorted in April 1980 to a military rescue mission, hoping to repeat the success of a brilliant Israeli commando raid that had freed 103 airline passengers at Entebbe, Uganda, in 1976. However, the operation was a humiliating failure, and eight U.S. service members were killed. Only in January 1981, after the overwhelming defeat of his reelection bid, did Carter achieve an agreement with the Iranians. The hostages were released on January 20, 1981, minutes after the inauguration of the new U.S. president, Ronald W. Reagan.

The Soviets in Afghanistan

Brzezinski's fears that the U.S.S.R. would take advantage of the arc of crisis seemed justified when the Soviet army invaded Afghanistan in 1979. It is likely, however, that the Soviets were responding to a crisis of their own rather than trying to exploit another's.

Remote and rugged Afghanistan had been an object of imperialist intrigue throughout the 19th and 20th centuries because of its vulnerable location between the Russian and British Indian empires. After 1955, with India and Pakistan independent, the Afghan government of Mohammad Daud Khan forged economic and military ties to the U.S.S.R. The monarchy was overthrown by Daud Khan in 1973 and was succeeded by a one-party state. The small Afghan Communist party, meanwhile, broke into factions, while a fundamentalist Muslim group began an armed insurrection in 1975. Daud Khan worked to lessen Afghanistan's dependence on Soviet and U.S. aid, and he reportedly had a heated disagreement with Brezhnev himself during a visit to Moscow in April 1977. Leftists in the Afghan officer corps, perhaps fearing a blow against themselves, murdered Daud Khan in April 1978 and pledged to pursue friendly relations with the U.S.S.R.

Thus Afghanistan, under the rule of Nur Mohammad Taraki, was virtually in the Soviet camp. When Taraki objected to a purge of the Afghan Cabinet, however, the leader of a rival faction, Hafizullah Amin, had him arrested and killed. These intramural Communist quarrels both embarrassed the Soviets and threatened to destabilize the Afghan regime in the face of growing Muslim resistance. In the fall of 1979 the Soviets built up their military strength across the border and hinted to American diplomats that they might feel obliged to intervene. On December 25, 1979, the Soviet army began its occupation, and two days later a coup d'état led to the murder of Amin and the installation of Babrak Karmal, a creature of the KGB who had been brought into the country by Soviet paratroops.

The Soviets would probably have preferred to work through a pliant native regime rather than invade Afghanistan, but Amin's behaviour and Moscow's unwillingness to risk a domestic overthrow of a Communist regime forced their hand. The invasion, therefore, appeared to be an application of the Brezhnev Doctrine and was all the more pressing given that the Central Asian provinces of the Soviet Union were also vulnerable to the rise of Islāmic fundamentalism. The United States was tardy in responding to the 1978 coup despite Carter's concern over the arc of crisis and the murder of the U.S. ambassador in Kabul in February 1979. At the same time, the Soviet invasion aroused American suspicions of a grand strategy aimed at seizing a warm-water port on the Indian Ocean and the oil of the Persian Gulf. Over the course of the next decade, however, the puppet Afghan regime lost all authority with the people, Afghan soldiers defected in large numbers, and the Muslim and largely tribal resistance, armed with U.S. and Chinese weapons, held out in the mountains against more than 100,000 Soviet troops and terror bombing of their villages. More than 2,000,000 Afghans became refugees in Pakistan and Iran. Western observers soon began to speak of Afghanistan as the Soviets' Vietnam.

The Iran-Iraq War Begins

The Shī'ite revolution in Iran, meanwhile, provoked and tempted neighbouring Iraq into starting yet another war in the arc of crisis. The secular Iraqi regime was nervous about the impact Iranian events might have on its own large Shī'ite population. The Kurdish minority, which had resorted to terrorism in pursuit of its goal of a Kurdish state to be carved out of Turkey, Iraq, and Iran, also presented an intractable problem. Finally, the Iraqi government of Saddam Hussein hoped to use the opportunity of Iran's apparent near-anarchy to seize the long-disputed Shaṭṭ al-'Arab waterway at the mouth of the Tigris-Euphrates river system. Bolstered by arms purchased with oil revenues, Hussein unilaterally abrogated a 1975 accord on the waterway and launched a full-scale invasion of Iran in September 1980.

After initial victories the Iraqis were surprisingly thrown back and a war of attrition commenced. The Iraqis employed poison gas and were building a nuclear reactor capable of producing weapons-grade plutonium until the Israeli air force destroyed the facility in a surprise raid in June 1981. The Iranians relied on human-wave assaults by revolutionary youths assured of a place in paradise for dying in battle.

Both sides employed imported planes and missiles to attack each other's oil facilities, tanker ships, and, occasionally, cities. Attacks then spread to neutral shipping as well, and oil production in the entire gulf region was placed in jeopardy. Neither superpower had direct interest in the war, except for a common opposition to any overthrow of the local balance of power, but the Soviets tended to benefit from a prolongation of the conflict. In 1987 the United States sharply increased its presence in the gulf by permitting Kuwaiti oil tankers to fly the U.S. flag and by deploying a naval task force to protect them in passage through the gulf. Compared to the situation of the 1950s, when John Foster Dulles' CENTO arrangement seemed to ensure a ring of stable, pro-Western governments in the South Asian region, that of the 1980s was almost totally unpredictable.

CHAPTER 6
RHETORICAL COLD WAR REVIVED

A s the 1980s opened, few predicted that it would be a decade of unprecedented progress in superpower relations. All pretense of détente had disappeared in 1979, and the election of 1980 brought to the White House a conservative Republican, Ronald Reagan, who was more determined to compete vigorously with the U.S.S.R. than any president had been since the 1960s. He bemoaned an "arms control process" that, he said, always favoured the Soviets and sapped the will of the Western allies and a détente that duped gullible Americans into acquiescing in unilateral Soviet gains.

Reagan sounded like Dulles when he denounced the Soviet Union as "an evil empire," and he echoed John F. Kennedy in calling for America to "stand tall" in the world again. Like Kennedy, he cut taxes in hopes of stimulating the stagnant U.S. economy, expanded the military budget (a process begun in Carter's last year), and stressed the development of sophisticated military technology beyond the means of the U.S.S.R. Reagan insisted that history was on the side of freedom, not Communism, and together with his close friend British Prime Minister Margaret Thatcher he sought to dispel the "malaise" that had afflicted the United States during the late 1970s. To be sure, Reagan had to work within the constraints caused by growing federal deficits, Soviet parity in nuclear arms, and congressional limits on executive action.

Hence his actual policies resembled more the cautious containment of the Eisenhower era than the aggressive interventionism of the Kennedy–Johnson years. The one novel means adopted by the administration for combatting Soviet power and influence was to extend aid to irregular forces engaged in resisting pro-Soviet governments in the Third World. Such "freedom fighters," as Reagan termed them, in Afghanistan, Angola, and Nicaragua seemed to offer hope that the United States could contain or even overthrow totalitarian regimes without getting itself involved in new Vietnams. This Reagan Doctrine was thus a natural corollary of the Nixon Doctrine.

Soviet Policy in the Early 1980s

As American diplomacy recovered its self-confidence and initiative, Soviet foreign policy drifted, if only because of the advanced age of Brezhnev and the frequent changes in leadership after his death in November 1982. Early in the decade a recurrence of serious unrest in eastern Europe, this time in Poland, also kept the attention of the Kremlin close to home. During the period of détente the Polish government had expanded an ambitious development plan financed largely by western European credits. Economic performance foundered, however, foreign debt mounted to $28,000,000,000, and the state imposed successive price hikes on staples.

By 1979–80 a popular protest movement had grown up around the officially unsanctioned Solidarity trade union and its charismatic leader, Lech Wałęsa. The strong Roman Catholic roots of Polish popular nationalism were evident in the movement, especially in light of the accession in 1978 of Karol Cardinal Wojtyła as Pope John Paul II, the first non-Italian pope in 456 years, who in 1981 survived an assassination plot probably hatched in Bulgaria, a Soviet satellite. As unrest mounted in Poland, NATO countries warned against a Soviet military intervention, holding in reserve the threat of declaring Warsaw in default on its debts. In December 1981, General Wojciech Jaruzelski declared martial law, sparing Poland a Soviet invasion at the price of military rule and the suppression of Solidarity. The United States responded by suspending Poland's most-favoured-nation trade status and blocking further loans from the International Monetary Fund. Reagan held the Soviet Union responsible for martial law; his attempts to extend the sanctions to an embargo on high-technology exports to the U.S.S.R., however, angered western Europeans, who feared losing access to eastern European markets and who were in the process of completing a huge pipeline from Siberia that would make western Europe dependent on the U.S.S.R. for 25 percent of its natural gas. In both the debt and pipeline issues, it seemed that the web of interdependence woven during détente served to constrain Western countries more than it did the U.S.S.R.

Brezhnev's successor as general secretary of the Communist Party, the former KGB chief Yury Andropov, declared that there was no alternative to détente as the Soviets understood it. He denounced Reagan's "militaristic course" as a new bid for U.S. hegemony. It was Reagan's image of the U.S.S.R., however, that seemed confirmed when a Soviet jet fighter plane shot down a civilian South Korean airliner in Soviet air space in September 1983, killing 269 people. Some in the West supported the Soviet claim that the plane was on a spy mission, but they produced no persuasive evidence to that effect. Andropov's demise after a year and a half elevated Konstantin Chernenko, another member of the older generation of the Politburo who would himself survive only until March 1985. Given these frequent changes in leadership and the drain on Soviet resources caused by the ongoing war in Afghanistan, the Kremlin was even less able than the White House to mount new initiatives in foreign policy until late in the 1980s.

SOLIDARITY

Solidarnos'c', or Solidarity, is a Polish trade union that in the early 1980s became the first independent labour union in a country belonging to the Soviet bloc. The origin of Solidarity traces back to 1976, when a Workers' Defense Committee (Komitet Obrony Robotnikow; KOR) was founded by a group of dissident intellectuals after several thousand striking workers had been attacked and jailed by authorities in various cities. The KOR supported families of imprisoned workers, offered legal and medical aid, and disseminated news through an underground network. In 1979 it published a Charter of Workers' Rights.

During a growing wave of new strikes in 1980 protesting rising food prices, Gdańsk became a hotbed of resistance to government decrees. Some 17,000 workers at the Lenin Shipyards there staged a strike and barricaded themselves within the plant under the leadership of Lech Wałęsa, an electrician by trade. In mid-August 1980 an Interfactory Strike Committee was established in Gdańsk to coordinate rapidly spreading strikes there and elsewhere; within a week it presented the Polish government with a list of demands that were based largely on KOR's Charter of Workers' Rights. On August 31, accords reached between the government and the Gdańsk strikers sanctioned free and independent unions with the right to strike, together with greater freedom of religious and political expression.

Solidarity formally was founded on Sept. 22, 1980, when delegates of 36 regional trade unions met in Gdańsk and united under the name Solidarnos'c'. The KOR subsequently disbanded, its activists becoming members of the union, and Wałęsa was elected chairman of Solidarity. A separate agricultural union composed of private farmers, named Rural Solidarity (Wiejska Solidarnos'c'), was founded in Warsaw on Dec. 14, 1980. By early 1981 Solidarity had a

Lech Wałęsa announces the end of the strike at the Lenin Shipyards on August 21, 1980.

membership of about 10 million people and represented most of the work force of Poland.

Throughout 1981 the government (led by General Wojciech Jaruzelski) was confronted by an ever stronger and more demanding Solidarity, which inflicted a series of controlled strikes to back up its appeals for economic reforms, for free elections, and for the involvement of trade unions in decision making at the highest levels. Solidarity's positions hardened as the moderate Wałęsa came to be pressured by more militant unionists. Jaruzelski's government, meanwhile, was subjected to severe pressure from the Soviet Union to suppress Solidarity.

On Dec. 13, 1981, Jaruzelski imposed martial law in Poland in a bid to crush the Solidarity movement. Solidarity was declared illegal, and its leaders were arrested. The union was formally dissolved by the Sejm (Parliament) on Oct. 8, 1982, but it nevertheless continued as an underground organization.

In 1988 a new wave of strikes and labour unrest spread across Poland, and prominent among the strikers' demands was government recognition of Solidarity. In April 1989 the government agreed to legalize Solidarity and allow it to participate in free elections to a bicameral Polish parliament. This was the first time an opposition movement had been allowed to participate in free elections in a Soviet bloc nation since the 1940s. In the elections, held in June of that year, candidates endorsed by Solidarity won 99 of 100 seats in the newly formed Senate (upper house) and all 161 seats (of 460 total) that opposition candidates were entitled to contest in the Sejm (lower house). In August Solidarity agreed to form a coalition government with Poland's United Workers' Party (PUWP), and a longtime Solidarity adviser, Tadeusz Mazowiecki, on August 24 became the first noncommunist premier to govern Poland since the late 1940s. In December 1990 Wałęsa was elected president of Poland after splitting with Mazowiecki in a dispute over the pace of Poland's conversion to a market economy. The split between Wałęsa and Mazowiecki prevented the formation of a Solidarity-backed coalition to govern the country in the wake of the PUWP's collapse, and the union's direct role in Poland's new parliamentary scene dwindled as many new political parties emerged in the early 1990s.

Renewal of Arms Control

The most serious consequence of the collapse of détente and the failure of the SALT II Treaty (judged by Reagan as "seriously flawed") appeared to be an acceleration of the arms race between the superpowers. Liberal critics feared that Reagan would unleash a new arms race; his supporters asserted that the Soviets had never stopped racing even during the era of SALT. Reagan waffled on arms policy, however, because of stiff domestic and European opposition to the abandonment of arms control.

Programs to upgrade the three elements of strategic deterrence were approved only after being cut back, yet they drew complaints from the Soviet Union that the highly accurate MX missile, the new Poseidon nuclear submarines, and air-launched cruise missiles for the B-52 force were first-strike weapons. A serious NATO worry stemmed from Soviet deployment of the new SS-20 theatre ballistic missile in Europe. In 1979 the Carter administration had acceded to the request by NATO governments that the United States introduce 572 Pershing II and cruise missiles into Europe to balance the 900 SS-20s. The European antinuclear movement, however, now officially patronized by the British Labour Party, the Greens in West Germany, and Dutch and Belgian social democrats, forced Reagan to link Pershing deployment with intermediate nuclear forces (INF) talks with the U.S.S.R. Reagan tried to seize the moral high ground with his "zero-option" proposal for complete elimination of all such missiles from Europe and a call for new Strategic Arms Reduction Talks (START) to negotiate real reductions in the superpower arsenals. The Soviets, however, refused to scrap any of their long-range missiles or to trade existing SS-20s for Pershings yet to be deployed.

In March 1983, Reagan announced a major new research program to develop antiballistic missile defenses based in outer space. This Strategic Defense Initiative (SDI, dubbed "Star Wars" by opponents) was inspired by the emergence of new laser and particle-beam technology that seemed to have the potential to devise an accurate, instantaneous, and nonnuclear means of shooting down long-range missiles in their boost phase, before their multiple reentry vehicles had a chance to separate. The president thus challenged his country to exploit its technological edge to counter the threat of Soviet offensive missiles and perhaps liberate the world from fear of a nuclear holocaust.

Scientific and political critics ridiculed SDI as naive (because it would not work or could be easily countered), expensive beyond reckoning, counterproductive (because it implied repudiation of the 1972 ABM Treaty), and dangerous (because the Soviets might stage a preemptive attack to prevent its deployment). The alarmed Soviets, however, weakened the case of American critics by launching their own propaganda campaign against SDI, implying that they took seriously its prospects for success. Evidence also mounted that the U.S.S.R. had been engaged in similar research since the mid-1970s. A $26,000,000,000, five-year American program was approved, although Congress limited future funding and arms-control advocates pressured the president to use SDI as a bargaining chip in the START talks. The Soviets broke off the INF and START talks at the end of 1983 but resumed talks two years later, apparently with hopes of stalling SDI research.

Crises in Africa and the Middle East

U.S.–Soviet competition in the Third World also continued through the 1980s as the Soviets sought to benefit from indigenous sources of unrest. The campaign of the

Communist-led African National Congress (ANC) against apartheid in South Africa, for instance, might serve Soviet strategic aims, but the black rebellion against white rule was surely indigenous. White-supremacist governments in southern Africa might argue, correctly, that the standard of living and everyday security of blacks were better in their countries than in most black-ruled African states, but the fact remained that African blacks, like all human beings, preferred to be ruled by their own tyrant rather than one of some other nationality or race. What was more, the respect shown by African governments for international boundaries began to break down after 1970. Spain's departure from the Spanish (Western) Sahara was the signal for a guerrilla struggle among Moroccan and Mauritanian claimants and the Polisario movement backed by Algeria. The Somali invasion of the Ogaden, Libyan intrusions into Chad and Sudan, and Uganda's 1978 invasion of Tanzania exemplified a new volatility. Uganda had fallen under a brutal regime headed by Idi Amin, whom most African leaders tolerated (even electing him president of the Organization of African Unity) until Julius Nyerere spoke out, following Uganda's invasion of his country, about the African tendency to reserve condemnation for white regimes only.

The black revolt against white rule in southern Africa was a timely consequence of the decolonization of Angola and Mozambique and of the Lancaster House accord under which white Southern Rhodesians accepted majority rule. This agreement led in 1980 to the full independence of Zimbabwe under Robert Mugabe, who in 1984 declared his intention to create a one-party Marxist state. South Africa tried to deflect global disgust with its apartheid system by setting up autonomous tribal "homelands" for blacks, but no other government recognized them. United States diplomacy sought quietly to promote a comprehensive settlement of South Africa's problems by pressuring Pretoria to release South West Africa (Namibia) and gradually dismantle apartheid in return for a Cuban evacuation of Angola and Mozambique. This policy of "constructive engagement," by which the U.S. State Department hoped to retain leverage over Pretoria, came under criticism every time a new black riot or act of white repression occurred. Critics demanded economic divestment from, and stringent sanctions against, South Africa, but supporters of the policy argued that sanctions would inflict disproportionate economic harm on South African blacks, drive the whites to desperation, and encourage violence that would strengthen the hand of Communist factions. Congressional pressure finally forced the administration to compromise on a package of sanctions in 1986, and U.S. firms began to pull out of South Africa.

The Middle East remained crisis-prone despite the Egyptian–Israeli peace. In 1978 an Arab summit in Baghdad pledged $400,000,000 to the PLO over the next 10 years. A comprehensive Middle East peace was stymied by the unwillingness of rejectionist Arab states to negotiate without the PLO and by the U.S.-Israeli refusal to negotiate with the PLO.

In June 1982 the Begin government determined to put an end to terrorist raids by forcibly clearing out PLO strongholds inside Lebanon. In fact the Israeli army advanced all the way to Beirut in a bitter campaign that entrenched Syrian occupation of the strategic al-Biqā valley and intensified what already amounted to a Lebanese' civil war among Palestinians, Muslims of various sects and allegiances, and Christian militiamen. The United States sent Marines to Beirut to facilitate the evacuation of the PLO, while it tried without success to piece together a coalition Lebanese government and induce the Israelis and Syrians to withdraw. In October 1983 terrorists blew up the U.S. Marine barracks, killing more than 200 Americans. The Middle East peace process begun by Kissinger and continued by Carter seemed to have unraveled by the late 1980s. Western governments tried to coordinate policies on terrorism, including a firm refusal to bargain with kidnappers, but concern for the lives of hostages and fear of future retaliation insidiously weakened their resolve. In October 1985, however, the Israeli air force dispatched planes to bomb the PLO headquarters in Tunis. When Libyan-supported terrorists planted bombs in airports in Rome and Vienna in December 1985 and in a discotheque in Berlin in April 1986, Reagan ordered U.S. jets to attack terrorist training camps and air-defense sites in Libya. The raid was applauded by the American public, and terrorist incidents did seem to decline in number over the following year. Qaddafi suffered another reverse in the spring of 1987 when French-supported Chadian troops drove the Libyan invaders from their country.

In the Persian Gulf the Reagan administration held publicly aloof from the war between Iraq and Iran. Intelligence that Shī ite terrorists were behind the kidnapping of Americans in Beirut, however, prompted the administration secretly to supply arms to Iran in return for help, never forthcoming, in securing the release of hostages. There was also a notion that such a deal might forge links to moderate Iranians in hopes of better relations in the event of the aged Khomeini's death. While the motives were humanitarian and strategic, this action directly contradicted the policy of shunning negotiations with terrorists that the United States had been urging on its allies. When the operation was exposed, the Reagan administration lost credibility with Congress and foreign governments alike.

Latin-American Upheavals

After a tour of Latin America in 1950, the American diplomat George Kennan wrote a memo despairing that the region would ever achieve a modest degree of economic dynamism, social mobility, or liberal politics. The culture itself was, in his view, inhospitable to middle-class values. As late as 1945 almost all the Latin-American republics were governed by landowning oligarchies allied with the church and army, while illiterate, apolitical masses produced the mineral and agricultural goods to be exported in exchange for manufactures from Europe and North America.

MARXISM AND THE CUBAN ROLE

To Castro and other radical intellectuals, a stagnant Latin America without strong middle classes was precisely suited for a Marxist, not a democratic, revolution. Before 1958 the United States—the "colossus to the north"—had used its influence to quell revolutionary disturbances, whether out of fear of Communism, to preserve economic interests, or to shelter strategic assets such as the Panama Canal. After Castro's triumph of 1959, however, the United States undertook to improve its own image through the Alliance for Progress and to distance itself from especially obnoxious authoritarian regimes. Nonetheless, Latin-American development programs largely failed to keep pace with population growth and inflation, and frequently they were brought to naught by overly ambitious schemes or official corruption.

By the 1980s the wealthiest and largest states like Brazil and Mexico faced a crushing burden of foreign debt. Neo-Marxist economists of the 1960s and '70s argued that even the more enlightened policies of the Kennedy and Johnson administrations kept Latin America in a condition of stifling dependence on American capital and markets and on world commodity prices. Some endorsed the demands of the Third World bloc in the UN for a "new world economic order," involving a massive shift of resources from the rich countries to the poor or the "empowerment" of the developing countries to control the terms of trade along the lines of OPEC. Others advocated social revolution to transform Latin states from within. At the same time the example of Cuba's slide into the status of a Communist satellite fully dependent on the U.S.S.R. revived the fear and suspicion with which Americans habitually regarded Third World revolutions.

Even after the Bay of Pigs invasion and the 1962 missile crisis, Cuba retained a certain autonomy in foreign policy, while the Soviets exhibited caution about employing their Cuban clients. Castro preferred to place himself among the ranks of Third World revolutionaries like Nasser, Nyerere, or Ghana's Kwame Nkrumah rather than follow slavishly the Moscow party line. He also elevated himself to leadership of the nonaligned nations. When relations between Havana and Moscow cooled temporarily in 1967–68, Brezhnev applied pressure, holding back on oil shipments and delaying a new trade agreement. Castro tried to resist the pressure by exhorting and mobilizing his countrymen to produce a record 10,000,000-ton sugar harvest in 1970. When the effort failed, Castro moved Cuba fully into the Soviet camp. The U.S.S.R. agreed to purchase 3,000,000 to 4,000,000 tons of sugar per year at four times the world price, provide cheap oil, and otherwise subsidize the island's economy at a rate of some $3,000,000,000 per year; thenceforward, 60 percent of Cuba's trade was with countries in the Soviet bloc. Brezhnev himself visited Cuba in 1974 and declared the country "a strong constituent part of the world system of Socialism." Castro, in turn, voiced the Soviet line on world issues, played host to Latin-American Communist party conventions, used the forum of the nonaligned nations movement to promote his distinctly aligned program, and made tens of thousands of Cuban troops available to support pro-Soviet regimes in Africa.

Soviet domination of Cuba, however, may have harmed their chances elsewhere in Latin America, since it alerted other leftists to the dangers of seeking Soviet support. Moreover, the Soviets simply could not afford such massive aid to other clients. This limitation appeared to be crucial even when Communists had a chance of prevailing in one of the largest, most developed South American states, Chile. The Communist party there was a charter member of the 1921 Comintern and had strong ties to the Chilean labour movement. The party was outlawed until 1956, whereupon it formed an electoral popular front with the Socialists, and it narrowly missed electing Socialist Salvador Allende Gossens to the presidency in 1964. The Christian Democratic opponent, Eduardo Frei Montalva, had warned that an Allende victory would make Chile "another Cuba."

From 1964 to 1970, when Cuba was plying an autonomous course, the Chilean Castroites staged violent strikes, bombings, and bank robberies in defiance of the regular Communist party directed from Moscow. The latter's strategy was subtler. Hinting that it might support the Christian Democratic candidate rather than rival leftists, the Communist party provoked the extreme right to run its own candidate in protest, thus splitting the conservative vote. The Nixon administration tried clumsily to influence the nominating process or foment a military coup, but Allende won an electoral victory in 1970. Once in office, he seized U.S. property and forged close ties to Cuba at the very time Castro was being reined in by Brezhnev. The U.S.S.R., however, held back from extending large-scale aid, even after a fall in copper prices, radical union activity, and Allende's policies had plunged Chile into economic chaos. In September 1973, General Augusto Pinochet Ugarte and the army overthrew Allende and established an authoritarian state. The Soviets and Allende sympathizers in North and South

America depicted the denouement in Chile as the work of Fascists in league with U.S. imperialists.

The poor image of the United States in Latin America was of special concern to Jimmy Carter because of his dedication to the promotion of human rights. During his first year in office Carter sought to counter the traditional notion of "Yankee imperialism" by meeting the demands of the Panamanian leader, General Omar Torrijos Herrera, for a transfer of sovereignty over the Panama Canal. The U.S. Senate ratified the treaty (which called for a staged transfer, to be completed in 1999) by a bare majority, but most Americans opposed transfer of the canal. Conservatives also held Carter's human rights concerns to be naive, because the linking of U.S. government loans, for instance, to a regime's performance on human rights damaged American relations with otherwise friendly states while exercising no influence on human rights practices in Communist states. Supporters of Carter retorted that the pattern of U.S. support for cruel oligarchies on the excuse of anti-Communism was what drove oppressed Latinos toward Communism in the first place.

The first hemispheric explosion in the 1980s, however, occurred in the southern cone of South America when the Argentine military ruler, Lieutenant General Leopoldo Galtieri—apparently to distract attention from the abuses of his dictatorship and an ailing economy at home—broke off talks concerning sovereignty over the Falkland Islands (Islas Malvinas) and invaded the remote archipelago in April 1982. The British government of Margaret Thatcher was taken by surprise but began at once to mobilize supplies, ships, and men to reconquer the islands some 8,000 miles from home. The United States was torn between loyalty to its NATO ally (and political friend of President Reagan) and the fear of antagonizing South Americans by siding with the "imperialists."

When U.S. diplomacy failed to resolve the dispute, however, the United States supplied Britain with intelligence data from American reconnaissance satellites. The Royal Navy and ground forces began operations in May, and the last Argentine defenders surrendered on June 14. In the wake of the defeat, the military junta in Buenos Aires gave way to democratization.

NICARAGUA AND EL SALVADOR

Problems in Central America, however, commanded the attention of the United States throughout the 1980s. In Nicaragua the broadly based Sandinista revolutionary movement challenged the oppressive regime of Anastasio Somoza Debayle, whose family had ruled the country since the 1930s. In accordance with its human rights policies, the Carter administration cut off aid to Somoza, permitting the Sandinistas to take power in 1979. They appeared to Americans as democratic patriots and received large sums of U.S. aid. A radical faction soon took control of the revolution, however, and moderates either departed or were forced out of the government in Managua. The Sandinistas then socialized the economy, suppressed freedom of the press and religion, and established close ties to Cuba and other Soviet-bloc countries. By the time Reagan took office, neighbouring El Salvador had also succumbed to violence among leftist insurgents, authoritarian landowners supporting right-wing death squads, and a struggling reformist government. Reagan vigorously affirmed a last-minute decision by Carter to grant military aid to the Salvadoran government. Although Nicaragua and Cuba were identified as the sources of the insurgency, Americans became increasingly confused by evidence of atrocities on all sides and were again torn between their desire to promote human rights and their determination to halt the spread of Communism. Opponents of U.S. involvement warned of another Vietnam in Central America, while supporters warned of another Cuba.

Nicaragua, meanwhile, built up one of the largest armies in the world in proportion to population, expanded its port facilities, and received heavy shipments of arms from the U.S.S.R. The CIA used this military buildup to justify the secret mining of Nicaraguan harbours in February 1984, which was, when revealed, universally condemned. The CIA also secretly organized and supplied a force of up to 15,000 anti-Sandinista "freedom fighters," known as Contras, across the border in Honduras and Costa Rica, while U.S. armed forces conducted joint maneuvers with those states along the Nicaraguan border. The ostensible purpose of such exercises was to interdict the suspected flow of arms from Nicaragua to the Salvadoran rebels. In fact, American policy aimed at provoking a popular revolt in hopes of overthrowing the Sandinistas altogether.

Cuban and Soviet influence with leftist governments on the Caribbean islands of Jamaica, Trinidad, and Grenada also appeared to be on the increase, a trend that the Reagan administration tried to counter with its 1982 Caribbean Basin Initiative, an Alliance for Progress confined to the islands. Grenada, a tiny island that had won independence from Britain in 1974, initially came under the control of Sir Eric Gairy, whose policies and conduct verged on the bizarre. In March 1979, Gairy was overthrown by the leftist New Jewel Movement led by the charismatic Maurice Bishop. Over the next several years the Bishop regime socialized the country, signed mutual-assistance agreements with Soviet-bloc states, and hastened construction of a large airstrip that the United States feared would ultimately be used by Soviet aircraft.

The evident incompetence of the New Jewel leadership, however, prompted a split in 1982 between Bishop's supporters and hard-line Leninists. In October 1983 the revolution came apart when Bishop was arrested and, when protest demonstrations broke out, shot. The Organization of East Caribbean States thereupon invited American intervention, and U.S. forces, together with small contingents from neighbouring islands, landed on Grenada to restore order and protect a group of American medical students. Free elections returned a moderate government to Grenada in 1984, but the self-destruction and overthrow of the New Jewel Movement, while a setback for Castroism in the region, also lent credence to Nicaragua's often and loudly voiced fear of an American invasion.

The U.S. public emphatically supported the Grenadan intervention but was split almost evenly on the question of support for the Nicaraguan Contras. While the Reagan Doctrine of supporting indigenous rebels, such as Savimbi's UNITA in Angola or the mujahideen in Afghanistan, appeared to be a low-risk means of countering Soviet influence, Americans remained nervous about the possibility of deeper U.S. involvement. Congress reflected this public ambivalence by first approving funds for the Contras, then restricting the ability of federal agencies to raise or spend funds for the Contras, then reversing itself again. In 1986 investigations of the secret U.S. arms sales to Iran revealed that National Security Council officials had kept supplies flowing to the Contras while the congressional restrictions were in effect by soliciting funds from private contributors and friendly Arab states and by diverting the profits from the Iranian arms sales.

In 1987 Congress launched lengthy investigations into the Iran-Contra Affair that virtually paralyzed U.S. foreign policy in the Middle East and Central America for more than a year. Reagan himself denied any knowledge of the secret arms sales and diversions of funds, although he granted that "mistakes had been made." Evidence emerged that William Casey, the director of the CIA, had known of the plan, but he died in May 1987. National Security Adviser John Poindexter and his aide, Lieutenant Colonel Oliver North, were eventually indicted for obstructing justice, although North's eloquent appeal to patriotism and anti-Communism in the televised hearings garnered much public support for the administration's ends, if not means.

In retrospect, the Iran-Contra Affair was another skirmish in the struggle between the executive and legislative branches over the conduct of foreign policy. Reagan and his advisers evidently believed, in light of the changed mood of the country after 1980 and his own electoral landslides, that they could revive the sort of vigorous intelligence and covert activities that the executive branch had engaged in before Vietnam and Watergate. The Democrats, who controlled both houses of Congress again after 1986, argued that covert operations subverted the separation of powers and the Constitution. The Iran-Contra Affair was especially obnoxious, in their view, because it contradicted the express policy not to deal with terrorists or governments that harboured them. The administration's defenders retorted that the United States would be impotent to combat terrorism and espionage without

Oliver North pleads the Fifth during preliminary hearings before the House Committee on Foreign Affairs in 1986.

strong and secret counterintelligence capabilities and that, since Congress had effectively hamstrung the CIA and too often leaked news of its activities, personnel of the National Security Council had taken matters into their own hands. The proper roles of the branches of the U.S. government in the formulation and execution of foreign policy thus remained a major source of bitterness and confusion after almost half a century of American leadership in global politics.

The World Political Economy

In 1980 the Soviet Union appeared to be stealing a march on a demoralized Western alliance through its arms buildup, occupation of Afghanistan, and influence with African and Central American revolutionaries, while the United States had been expelled from Iran and was suffering from inflation and recession at home. Eight years later the Reagan administration had rebuilt American defenses, presided over the longest peacetime economic expansion in 60 years, and regained the initiative in superpower relations. Because the "Reagan Revolution" in foreign and domestic policy was purchased through limits on new taxes even as military and domestic spending increased, the result was annual federal deficits measured in the hundreds of billions of dollars and financed only by the influx of foreign capital. Once the world's creditor, the United States became the world's biggest debtor. Moreover, American economic competitiveness declined to the point that U.S. trade deficits surpassed $100,000,000,000 per year, owing mostly to American imports of oil and of Japanese and German manufactured goods.

The sudden collapse of prices on the New York Stock Exchange in October 1987 compelled the White House and Congress alike to address the issue of American "decline." In

1988 Paul Kennedy, a Yale professor of British origin, published the best-seller *The Rise and Fall of the Great Powers*. He developed the thesis that a great state tends to overextend itself in foreign and defense policy during its heyday and thereby acquires vital interests abroad that soon become a drain on its domestic economy. Over time, new economic competitors unburdened by imperial responsibilities rise to challenge and eventually replace the old hegemonic power. It certainly seemed that the United States was such a power in decline: Its share of gross world production had fallen from almost 50 percent in the late 1940s to less than 25 percent, while Japan and West Germany had completed their postwar economic miracles and were still growing at a faster rate than the United States, even during the Reagan prosperity. New light industries, such as microelectronics, and even old heavy industries like steel and automobiles had spread to countries with skilled but relatively low-paid labour, such as South Korea, Taiwan, Hong Kong, and Singapore. Financial power had fled to new global banking centres in Europe and East Asia. In the 1960s, 9 of the 10 biggest banks in the world were American; by 1987 none were American, and most were Japanese.

These trends were in part natural, as other industrial regions recovered from their devastation in World War II and new ones arose. Whether natural or not, however, they seemed to indicate that the United States could no longer afford to uphold either the liberal trade environment it had founded after World War II or the worldwide responsibilities that devolved upon the "leader of the free world."

European growth, led as always by the dynamic West German economy, also signalled a change in the global distribution of power. Yet, even as the European Community (EC) expanded in terms of both production and size (Greece became its 10th member in 1981), it failed to demonstrate unity and political leverage commensurate with its economic might. For years EC officials, the so-called Eurocrats, had quarreled with member governments and among themselves over whether and how Europe should seek deeper as well as broader integration. Finally, in 1985, Jacques Delors, president of the European Commission, steered through the European Parliament in Strasbourg the Single European Act, which set 1992 as the target date for a complete economic merger of the EC countries, for a single European currency, and for common EC foreign and domestic policies: in short, a United States of Europe.

The immediate result was a seemingly endless round of haggling among European cabinets about this or that point of the 1992 plan. Was the abolition of the venerable pound sterling, the French franc, and the deutsche mark in favour of the ecu (European currency unit) really necessary? Could all member states coordinate their labour and welfare policies, or be willing to countenance the free movement of peoples across national borders? Would national governments in fact prove willing to relinquish part of their sovereignty in matters of justice, defense, and foreign policy? The moderate governments of the Christian Democrat Helmut Kohl in West Germany and Socialist President François Mitterrand in France, as well as those of Italy and the smaller countries, remained committed to "1992." Only Thatcher of the United Kingdom voiced doubts about merging Britain into a continental superstate. The alternative, however, would seem to leave Britain out in the cold, and so, despite Thatcher's opposition, plans for European unity went ahead. (In 1990, members of Thatcher's own party forced her resignation over the issue.)

Why did Europe resume the long-stalled drive for a more perfect union only in the mid-1980s? Some of the reasons are surely internal, having to do with the activities of the Eurocrats and the proclivities of the member governments. External factors also must have been important, including the debate over whether to base American missiles in Europe; the whole question of arms control, which affected Europe most directly but over which it had limited influence; widespread disaffection in Europe with Carter and (for different reasons) Reagan and hence a desire for a stronger European voice in world politics; and, last but not least, the Europeans' concern over the influx of Japanese manufactures. The world appeared by the late 1980s to be moving away from the ideals of national sovereignty and universal free trade and toward a contradictory reality in which international dependence increased at the same time that regional and increasingly competitive economic blocs coalesced.

To many analysts it seemed that the Cold War was simply becoming obsolete, that military power was giving way to economic power in world politics, and that the bipolar system was fast becoming a multipolar one including Japan, a united Europe, and China. Indeed, China, though starting from a low base, demonstrated the most rapid economic growth of all in the 1980s under the market-oriented reforms of the chairman Deng Xiaoping and Premier Li Peng. Paul Kennedy and many other analysts concluded that the United States could simply no longer afford the Cold War and would have to end it just to maintain itself against the commercial and technological competition of its own allies. For the U.S.S.R., the Cold War had to end if it was to maintain itself as a Great Power at all.

Disengagement in the Third World

The three main arenas of Cold War competition had always been divided Europe, strategic nuclear arms competition, and regional conflicts in the Third World. By the end of 1990 the superpowers had seemingly pacified the first arena, made substantial progress in the second, and at least stated their intention of disengaging in the third. Ever since the 1950s, when the U.S.S.R. first bid for allies and client states in Africa, Asia, and Latin America, the superpowers had wrestled for influence through programs of military and economic assistance, propaganda, and proxy wars in which they backed opposing states or factions. When Gorbachev came to power, the Soviets still possessed patron–client relationships with North Korea, Vietnam, Ethiopia, Angola, Cuba, Nicaragua, and Afghanistan and exercised considerable influence with Iraq, Syria, Yemen (Aden), and the frontline states confronting white-ruled South Africa. Moreover, the United States faced opposition to friendly regimes in the Philippines, El Salvador, and, of course, Israel. The Soviet Union's financial crisis increasingly limited its ability to underwrite client states, however, while its troubles in eastern Europe and at home afforded the United States the opportunity to resolve regional conflicts to its liking. Thus, events in disparate theatres of the world in the last half of the 1980s added up to a certain disengagement and reduction of Cold War–related tensions in the Third World.

THE PHILIPPINES AND CENTRAL AMERICA

In 1986 the corrupt autocrat of the Philippines, Ferdinand Marcos, a long-standing ally of the United States, lost his grip on power. Crowds backed by leading elements in the Roman Catholic church, the press, labour unions, and a portion of the army rose up to demand his resignation. The Reagan administration, like previous U.S. administrations, had tolerated Marcos in light of his determined opposition to the Communist guerrilla movement in the Philippines and his support for two major U.S. military bases on the island of Luzon. It now had to decide, however, whether Marcos' continued rule might in fact strengthen the appeal of anti-American leftists. In hopes of avoiding "another Iran" (referring to President Carter's abandonment of the Shah, only to see him replaced by the Ayatollah), Reagan sent a personal envoy to Manila to engineer Marcos' departure in favour of free elections and the accession to power of Corazon Aquino, the widow of a popular opposition leader who had been murdered. The United States had evidently managed to remove an embarrassing dictator without doing serious harm to its strategic position in East Asia.

Closer to home, the United States continued to face not only the aggressively hostile Sandinista regime in Nicaragua and the leftist rebellion in El Salvador (backed, the White House said, by Nicaragua, Cuba, and the Soviet Union) but also a growing rift with the Panamanian dictator General Manuel Noriega. For decades Noriega had collaborated with U.S. intelligence agencies, serving as an informant on events in Cuba and a supporter of the Contras in Central America. It came to light, however, that in addition to grabbing all power in Panama he had amassed a personal fortune by smuggling illegal drugs into the United States, and in 1988 a U.S. grand jury indicted Noriega on drug-trafficking charges. The Reagan administration offered to drop the charges if Noriega would agree to step down and leave Panama, but he refused.

In May 1989, Panama staged elections monitored by an international team that included former U.S. President Carter. Although the opposition civilian candidate, Guillermo Endara, appeared to win by a 3-to-1 margin, Noriega annulled the vote, declared his own puppet candidate the victor, and had Endara and other opponents beaten in the streets. President Bush dispatched 2,000 additional soldiers to U.S. bases in the Panama Canal Zone, and the Organization of American States (OAS) called for a "peaceful transfer of power" to an elected govern-ment in Panama. In December 1989, Noriega bade the Panamanian National Assembly to name him "maximum leader" and declare a virtual "state of war" with the United States. Within days a U.S. soldier was ambushed and killed in Panama, an incident followed by the shooting of a Panamanian soldier by U.S. military guards.

President Bush now considered that he had a pretext to act. A Panamanian judge taking refuge in the Canal Zone swore in Endara as president, and 24,000 U.S. troops (including 11,000 airlifted from the United States) seized control of Panama City. Noriega eluded the invaders for four days, then took refuge with the papal nuncio. On January 3, 1990, he surrendered himself to U.S. custody and was transported to Miami to stand trial. The OAS voted 20 to 1 to condemn what seemed to many Latin Americans an unwarranted "Yanqui" intervention.

The U.S. conflict with the Nicaraguan revolutionary regime of Daniel Ortega also reached a climax in 1989. On February 14 five Central American presidents, inspired by the earlier ini-tiatives of the Costa Rican president and Nobel Peace laureate Óscar Arias Sánchez, agreed to plans for a cease-fire in the

Manuel Noriega (center) *on the plane that took him to Miami to be tried on drug trafficking charges.*

entire region, the closing of Contra bases in Honduras, and monitored elections in Nicaragua to be held no later than February 1990. In April Nicaragua's National Assembly approved the plan and passed laws relaxing the Sandinistas' prohibitions of free speech and opposition political parties. Because the Sandinistas' prospects for continued, large-scale aid from Cuba and the U.S.S.R. were slim in light of the Soviet "new thinking," Ortega concluded that he must, after all, risk the fully free elections he had avoided ever since his takeover 10 years before. The five Central American presidents announced in August their schedule for the demobilization of the Contras, and in October the U.S. Congress acceded to Bush's request for nonmilitary aid to the Nicaraguan opposition.

The elections were held on February 25, 1990, and, to the surprise of almost everyone on both sides of the struggle, the Nicaraguan people favoured National Opposition Union leader Violeta Barrios de Chamorro by 55 to 40 percent. Ortega acknowledged his defeat and pledged to "respect and obey the popular mandate." The United States immediately suspended the aid to the Contras, lifted the economic sanctions against Nicaragua, and proposed to advance economic assistance to the new regime.

AFGHANISTAN

The resolution of regional conflicts at the end of the 1980s extended to Asia as well. In Afghanistan the Soviet Union had committed some 115,000 troops in support of the KGB-installed regime of President Mohammad Najibullah but had failed to eliminate the resistance of the mujahideen. The war became a costly drain on the Soviet budget and a blow to Soviet military prestige. In the atmosphere of glasnost even an antiwar movement of sorts arose in the Soviet Union. A turning point came in mid-1986, when the United States began to supply the Afghan rebels with surface-to-air Stinger missiles, which forced Soviet aircraft and helicopters to suspend their low-level raids on rebel villages and strongholds. In January 1987 Najibullah announced a cease-fire, but the rebels refused his terms and the war continued.

In February 1988 Gorbachev conceded the need to extract Soviet forces from the stalemated conflict. In April, Afghan, Pakistani, and Soviet repre-sentatives in Geneva agreed to a disengagement plan based on Soviet withdrawal by February 1989 and nonin-volvement in each other's internal affairs. The Soviets completed the evacuation on schedule but continued to supply the Kabul regime with large quantities of arms and supplies. The regime aban-doned its strategy of seeking out the mujahideen and instead pulled back into strong defensive bastions in the fertile valleys, maintain-ing control of roads and cities. The rebels lacked the tanks and artillery to launch major offensive operations, and internal feuds among the rebel leaders also inhibited their operations. Thus, the pre-dictions of Western journalists

Mujahideen rebels in eastern Afghanistan in February 1980.

that Kabul would soon fall were proved wrong; the Soviets' client state in Afghanistan survived into the 1990s.

THE IRAN-IRAQ WAR ENDS

The war between Iraq and Iran, which began in 1980, also reached a conclusion. The war had been conducted with the utmost ferocity on both sides. The Iraqi leader, Hussein, employed every weapon in his arsenal, including Soviet Scud missiles and poison gas purchased from West Germany, and the Iranian regime of Ayatollah Khomeini ordered its Revolutionary Guards to make human-wave assaults against fortified Iraqi positions. Total casualties in the conflict numbered in the hundreds of thousands. The Soviets and Americans remained aloof from the conflict but tilted toward Iraq. The primary Western (and Japanese) interests were to preserve a balance of power in the Persian Gulf and to maintain the free flow of oil from Kuwait, Saudi Arabia, and the emirates. In May 1987, after two Iraqi missiles struck a U.S. naval vessel in the gulf, the United States announced an agreement with Kuwait to reflag 11 Kuwaiti tankers and assign the U.S. Navy to escort them through the dangerous waters. Western European states and the U.S.S.R. deployed minesweepers.

The Iran–Iraq War entered its final phases in February 1988, when Hussein ordered the bombing of an oil refinery near Tehrān. The Iranians retaliated by launching missiles into Baghdad, and this "war of the cities" continued for months. In March, with the front stalemated along the Shaṭṭ al-ʿArab waterway, dissident Kurdish populations in the north of Iraq took advantage of the war to agitate for autonomy. Hussein struck back at the Kurds in genocidal fashion, bombing their villages with chemical weapons and poison gas. In May 1988 Iraq launched a massive surprise attack that drove the Iranians out of the small wedge of Iraqi territory they had occupied 16 months earlier, and after eight years of warfare the two sides were back where they started. Although Khomeini called the decision "more deadly than taking poison," he instructed his government to accept UN Resolution 598 calling for an immediate cease-fire and withdrawal to prewar boundaries. Iraq refused, and Hussein ordered a final air and ground offensive with extensive use of poison gas. The Iraqis advanced 40 miles into Iran. UN Secretary-General Javier Pérez de Cuéllar persevered in talks with the foreign ministers of the belligerents and announced finally that the two sides had agreed to a cease-fire beginning August 20, 1988.

To outsiders, Khomeini's militant Shī'ite regime in Tehrān appeared to be the most extreme, irrational, and dangerous government in the region. In fact, it was the secular revolutionary tyranny of Hussein that had begun the war and harboured the aggressive aims of seizing the mouth of the Tigris-Euphrates river system and establishing Iraq as the hegemonic power in the Persian Gulf. Iraq had assumed the strategic offensive, escalated the war, and initiated the use of weapons of indiscriminate mass destruction imported from Western and Soviet-bloc states alike.

THE INTIFADAH

In all these regions of the world long-standing conflicts either dissipated or lost their Cold War significance in the years 1986–90. One conflict, however, always remained volatile—and perhaps even more so for the retreat of the superpowers and their stabilizing influence: the conflict between Israel and the Palestinians. Throughout his years as U.S. secretary of state, George Schultz had tried to promote the peace process in the Middle East by brokering direct negotiations between Israel and the Palestine Liberation Organization. Such talks would require the PLO to renounce terrorism and recognize Israel's right to exist, but the PLO (which the Israeli ambassador Abba Eban said "never misses an opportunity to miss an opportunity") refused to make the requisite concessions.

In December 1987, Israeli soldiers in the Gaza Strip killed an Arab youth engaged in a protest. Widespread unrest broke out in the Israeli-occupied territories, leading to 21 deaths in two weeks. This was the start of the *intifāḍah* ("shaking"), a wave of Palestinian protests and Israeli reprisals that lent new urgency to Middle East diplomacy. Israeli military rule of the West Bank then hardened, and the Fatah faction of the PLO stepped up its terrorism from bases in Lebanon.

A first apparent breakthrough for U.S. policy occurred in November 1988, when the Palestine National Council, meeting in Algiers, voted overwhelmingly to accept UN Resolutions 242 and 338, calling for Israel to evacuate the occupied territories and for all countries in the region "to live in peace within secure and recognized boundaries." Did this imply PLO recognition of Israel's right to exist? At first the PLO chairman, Yasser Arafat, refused to say, whereupon the United States denied him a visa to make a trip to the UN. He did in fact speak to a reconvened UN in Geneva but again failed to be explicit about PLO policy. The next day, in a news conference, Arafat finally recognized Israel's right to exist, and he renounced terrorism as well. Schultz immediately announced that the United States would conduct "open dialogue" with the PLO. The Israelis, then in the midst of a cabinet crisis, were unable to respond decisively.

In March the new Israeli foreign minister, Moshe Arens, visited Washington, by which time the new Bush administration was also ready to make its first foray into the Arab Israeli thicket with a plan for liberalized Israeli rule on the West Bank in return for PLO action to moderate the intifadah and suspend raids on Israel from Lebanon. The Israelis had a plan of their own based on elections in the occupied territories, but without PLO participation or international observation. The Arab League endorsed the idea for a peace conference and held that Palestinian elections on the West Bank could occur only after an Israeli withdrawal. The Israeli prime minister, Yitzhak Shamir, retorted that elections could occur only after the intifadah had ended, insisted on continuing Israeli settlement on the West Bank, and denied the possibility of ever creating a Palestinian state. The deadlock in the Middle East was thus as intractable as ever.

In fact, the situation had hardened in the late 1980s for a variety of reasons. First, the Arabs themselves were seriously divided. Egypt, the most populous Arab state, had no desire to disturb its peace with Israel dating from the Camp David Accords. Saudi Arabia and the other wealthy oil states were preoccupied with the Persian Gulf crisis and nervous about the presence in their countries of thousands of Palestinian guest workers. Syria's president, Ḥafiz al-Assad, a bitter rival of Saddam Hussein, was busy absorbing a large chunk of Lebanon. King Hussein of Jordan was caught between Syria and Iraq, a prisoner of his large Palestinian refugee population, and yet in no condition to challenge Israel militarily. Meanwhile, the liberalization of emigration policy in the U.S.S.R. and the pervasive anti-Semitism there led to the influx of tens of thousands of Soviet Jews, whom the Israelis began to settle on the West Bank. Finally, the fading of the Cold War did little to enhance the ability of the superpowers to impose or broker a settlement in the region. Gorbachev hoped to improve relations with Israel while maintaining the Soviets' traditional ties to the radical Arab states and at the same time doing nothing to damage his détente with the United States. The Americans wanted to maintain their alliance with Israel but could not afford to alienate—or compromise—the moderate Arab governments so important to the stability of the oil-rich gulf.

CHAPTER 7

THE END OF THE COLD WAR

I n retrospect, the course of the Cold War appears to have been cyclical, with both the United States and the U.S.S.R. alternating between periods of assertion and relaxation. In the first years after 1945 the United States hastily demobilized its wartime military forces while pursuing universal, liberal internationalist solutions to problems of security and recovery. Stalin, however, rejected American blueprints for peace, exploited the temporarily favourable correlation of forces to impose Communist regimes on east-central Europe, and maintained the military-industrial emphasis in Soviet central planning despite the ruination done to his own country by the German invasion.

Soviet policy prompted the first American outpouring of energy, between 1947 and 1953, when the strategy of containment and policies to implement it emerged: the Truman Doctrine, the Marshall Plan, NATO, the Korean War, and the buildup in conventional and nuclear arms. Then the Americans tired; Eisenhower accepted a stalemate in Korea, cut defense spending, and opened a dialogue with Moscow in hopes of putting a lid on the arms race. Khrushchev then launched a new Soviet offensive in 1957, hoping to transform Soviet triumphs in space and missile technology into gains in Berlin and the Third World. The United States again responded, from 1961 to 1968 under Kennedy and Johnson, with another energetic campaign that ranged from the Apollo Moon program and nuclear buildup to the Peace Corps and counterinsurgency operations culminating in the Vietnam War. The war bogged down, however, and brought on economic distress and social disorder at home.

After 1969 Presidents Nixon and Ford scaled back American commitments, withdrew from Vietnam, pursued arms control treaties, and fostered détente with the U.S.S.R., while President Carter, in the wake of Watergate, went even further in renouncing Cold War attitudes and expenditures. It was thus that the correlation of forces again shifted in favour of the Soviet bloc, tempting Brezhnev in the 1970s to extend Soviet influence and power to its greatest extent and allowing the U.S.S.R. to equal or surpass the preoccupied United States in nuclear weapons.

After 1980, under Reagan, the United States completed the cycle with a final, self-confident assertion of will—and this time, the Soviets appeared to break. In May 1981, at Notre Dame University, the recently inaugurated Reagan predicted that the years ahead would be great ones for the cause of freedom and that Communism was "a sad, bizarre chapter in human history whose last pages are even now being written." At the time few took his words for more than a morale-boosting exhortation, but in fact the Soviet economy and polity were under terrific stress in the last Brezhnev years, though the Soviets did their best to hide the fact. They were running hidden budget deficits of 7 or 8 percent of GNP, suffering from extreme inflation that took the form (because of price controls) of chronic shortages of consumer goods, and falling farther behind the West in computers and other technologies vital to civilian and military performance.

The Reagan administration recognized and sought to exploit this Soviet economic vulnerability. Secretary of Defense Caspar Weinberger and his aide Richard Perle tightened controls on the export of strategic technologies to the Soviet bloc.

CIA Director William Casey persuaded Saudi Arabia to drive down the price of oil, thereby denying the U.S.S.R. billions of dollars it expected to glean from its own petroleum exports. The United States also pressured its European allies to cancel or delay the massive pipeline project for the importation of natural gas from Siberia, thereby denying the Soviets another large source of hard currency.

Such economic warfare, waged at a time when the Soviet budget was already strained by the Afghan war and a renewed strategic arms race, pushed the Soviet economy to the brink of collapse. Demoralization took the form of a growing black market, widespread alcoholism, the highest abortion rate in the world, and a declining life span. In an open society such symptoms might have provoked protests and reforms, leadership changes, possibly even revolution. The totalitarian state, however, thoroughly suppressed civil society, while even the Communist party, stifled by its jealous and fearful *nomenklatura* (official hierarchy), was incapable of adjusting. In sum, the Stalinist methods of terror, propaganda, and mass exploitation of labour and resources had served well enough to force an industrial revolution in Russia, but they were inadequate to the needs of the postindustrial world.

Gorbachev and the Soviet "New Thinking"

Young, educated, and urban members of the Communist elite came gradually to recognize the need for radical change if the Soviet Union was to survive, much less hold its own with the capitalist world. They waited in frustration as Brezhnev was followed by Andropov, then by Chernenko. The reformers finally rose to the pinnacle of party leadership, however, when Mikhail Gorbachev was named general secretary in 1985. A lawyer by training and a loyal Communist, Gorbachev did not begin his tenure by urging a relaxation of the Cold War. He stressed economics instead: a crackdown on vodka consumption, laziness, and "hooliganism" said to be responsible for "stagnation"; and, when that failed, a far-reaching perestroika, or restructuring, of the economy. It was in connection with this economic campaign that surprising developments in foreign policy began to occur. Not only were the costs of empire—the military, KGB and other security agencies, subsidies to foreign client states—out of all proportion to the Soviet GNP, but the U.S.S.R., no less than in earlier times, desperately needed Western technology and credits in order to make up for its own backwardness. Both to trim the costs of empire and to gain Western help, Gorbachev had to resolve outstanding disputes abroad and tolerate more human rights at home.

As early as 1985 the "new thinking" of the younger Communist apparatchiks began to surface. Gorbachev declared that no nation's security could be achieved at the expense of another's—an apparent repudiation of the goal of nuclear and conventional superiority for which the Soviets had worked for so long. Soviet historians began to criticize Brezhnev's policies toward Afghanistan, China, and the West and to blame him, rather than "capitalist imperialism," for the U.S.S.R.'s encirclement. In 1986 Gorbachev said that economic power had supplanted military power as the most important aspect of security in the present age—an amazing admission for a state whose superpower status rested exclusively on its military might. He called on the Soviets to settle for "reasonable sufficiency" in strategic arms and urged NATO to join him in deep cuts in nuclear and conventional weapons. He reiterated Khrushchev's remark that nuclear war could have no winners and de Gaulle's vision of a "common European house" from the Atlantic Ocean to the Ural Mountains. Finally, Gorbachev hinted at a repudiation of the Brezhnev Doctrine—*i.e.*, the assertion of the Soviets' right to intervene to protect Socialist governments wherever they might be threatened.

Western observers were divided at first as to how to respond to this "new thinking." Some analysts considered Gorbachev a revolutionary and his advent a historic chance to end the Cold War. Others, including the Reagan administration, were more cautious. Soviet leaders had launched "peace offensives" many times before, always with the motive of seducing the West into opening up trade and technology. Gorbachev was a phenomenon, charming Western reporters, crowds, and leaders (Thatcher was especially impressed) with his breezy style, sophistication, and peace advocacy. He published two best-sellers in the West to enhance his reputation, which for a time caused Europeans to rate Reagan and the United States the greatest threats to peace in the world. What convinced most Western observers that genuine change had occurred, however, was not what Gorbachev said but what he allowed others to say under his policy of glasnost, or openness.

As Western experts had predicted, perestroika, an attempt to streamline a fatally flawed Communist system, was doomed to failure. What the Soviets needed, they said, was a profit motive, private property, hard currency, real prices, and access to world markets. But Gorbachev, still thinking in Communist categories, blamed bureaucratic resistance for the failure of his reforms and thus declared glasnost to encourage internal criticism. What he got was the birth of a genuine Soviet public opinion, a reemergence of autonomous organizations in society, and more than 300 independent journals (by the end of 1989) publicizing and denouncing Communist military and economic failures, murder and oppression, foreign policy "crimes" such as the German-Soviet Nonaggression Pact and the invasion of Afghanistan, and even Communist rule itself.

By 1987 most Western observers still called for deeds to match the words pouring forth in the Soviet Union, but they were persuaded that an end to the Cold War was a real possibility. On June 12, 1987, during a visit to Berlin, Reagan gave a memorable speech at the Brandenburg Gate that directly challenged his Soviet counterpart to back up his reforms with actions, declaring, "General Secretary Gorbachev, if you seek peace, if you seek prosperity for the Soviet Union and Eastern Europe, if you seek liberalization: Come here to this gate! Mr. Gorbachev, open this gate! Mr. Gorbachev, tear down this wall!"

The Reagan administration made its first show of trust in Gorbachev by engaging in negotiations to eliminate nuclear weapons from Europe. In 1987 Gorbachev surprised the United States by accepting the earlier American "zero-option" proposal for intermediate-range missiles. After careful negotiation a treaty was concluded in Geneva and signed at a Washington summit in December. This controversial Intermediate-Range Nuclear Forces (INF) Treaty eliminated an entire class of nuclear weapons and allowed, for the first time, extensive on-site inspection inside the Soviet bloc. Critics still feared that stripping Europe of nuclear missiles might only enhance the value of the Soviets' conventional superiority and called for parallel agreements through the mutual and balanced force reduction talks on NATO and Warsaw Pact armies. In Moscow in mid-1988, Reagan and Gorbachev discussed an even bolder proposal: reduction of both strategic nuclear arsenals by 50 percent. A mellower Reagan, interpreting the Soviets' new flexibility as a vindication of his earlier tough stance and having thereupon repudiated his "evil empire" rhetoric, now seemed eager to bargain as much as possible with Gorbachev.

Finally, Gorbachev and his foreign minister, Eduard Shevardnadze, reached out in all directions—China, Japan,

Reagan and Gorbachev sign the INF treaty on Dec. 8, 1987.

India, Iran, even South Korea and Israel—in hopes of reducing military tensions, gaining access to trade and technology, or just creating new possibilities for Soviet statecraft. Gorbachev's most celebrated moment came in December 1988 at the United Nations, when he announced a unilateral reduction in Soviet army forces of half a million men and the withdrawal from eastern Europe of 10,000 tanks. Henceforth, he said, the U.S.S.R. would adopt a "defensive posture," and he invited the NATO countries to do the same.

Throughout his first four years in power Gorbachev inspired and presided over an extraordinary outpouring of new ideas and new options. Western skeptics wondered whether he meant to dismantle Communism and the Soviet empire and, if he did, whether he could possibly avoid being overthrown by party hard-liners, the KGB, or the army. He had maneuvered brilliantly in internal politics, always claiming the middle ground and positioning himself as the last best hope for peaceful reform. His prestige and popularity in the West were also assets of no small value. In June 1988 he persuaded the Communist party conference to restructure the entire Soviet government along the lines of a partially representative legislature with a powerful president—himself. Was the Gorbachev phenomenon merely an updated version of earlier, limited Russian and Soviet reforms designed to bolster the old order? Or would Gorbachev use his expanding power to liquidate the empire and Communism?

In truth, Gorbachev faced a severe dilemma born of three simultaneous crises: diplomatic encirclement abroad, economic and technological stagnation at home, and growing pressure for liberal reform in Poland and Hungary and for autonomy in the non-Russian republics of the U.S.S.R. Thoroughgoing détente, perhaps even an end to the Cold War, could solve the first crisis and go far toward ameliorating the second. His policy of glasnost, deemed vital to economic progress, had the fatal side effect, however, of encouraging repressed ethnic groups, at home and in eastern Europe, to organize and express their opposition to Russian or Communist rule. Of course, the Soviet government might simply crush the nationalities, as it had in Hungary in 1956 and Czechoslovakia in 1968, but that in turn would undo the progress made in East–West relations and put Gorbachev back where he had started. If, on the other hand, the Soviet government relinquished its satellites abroad, how could it stop the process of liberation from spreading to the subject nationalities inside the U.S.S.R.? If it repudiated its Marxist-Leninist global mission in the name of economic reform, how could the regime legitimize itself at all, even in Russia?

Liberalization and Struggle in the Soviet Bloc

George Bush was elected to succeed Ronald Reagan as president of the United States in November 1988. The new administration's foreign policy team, led by Secretary of State James Baker, was divided at first between the "squeezers," who saw no logic in attempts to bail out a troubled Soviet Union, and the "dealers," who wanted to make far-reaching agreements with Gorbachev before he was toppled from power. For five months Bush played his cards close to his vest, citing the need to await the results of a comprehensive study of Soviet–American relations.

Signs of unmistakable and irreversible liberalization in the Soviet bloc began to appear in the form of popular manifestations in eastern Europe, which the Kremlin seemed willing to tolerate and even, to some extent, encourage. Czechoslovaks demonstrated against their Communist regime on the anniversary of the 1968 Soviet invasion. In Poland, the Solidarity union demanded democratic reforms. The Sejm (parliament) legalized and vowed to return the property of the Roman Catholic church, and the government of General Jaruzelski approved partially free elections to be held on June 4, 1989, the first such in over 40 years. Solidarity initially won 160 of the 161 available seats and then took the remaining seat in a runoff election, effectively becoming the first Soviet satellite state to renounce Communism and declare independence. On May 2, Hungary dismantled barriers on its border with Austria—the first real breach in the Iron Curtain.

Gorbachev was less tolerant of protests and separatist tendencies in the U.S.S.R. itself; for instance, he ordered soldiers to disperse 15,000 Georgians demanding independence. He moved ahead, however, with reforms that loosened the Communist party's grip on power in the Soviet Union, even as his own authority was increased through various laws granting him emergency powers. In March, protesters in Moscow supported the parliamentary candidacy of the dissident Communist Boris Yeltsin, who charged Gorbachev with not moving fast enough toward democracy and a market economy. On the 26th of that month, in the first relatively free elections ever held in the Soviet Union, for 1,500 of the 2,250 seats in the new Congress of People's Deputies, various non-Communists and ethnic representatives emerged triumphant over Communist party candidates. Three days later Gorbachev told the Hungarian premier that he opposed foreign intervention in the internal affairs of Warsaw Pact states—a loud hint that he did not intend to enforce the Brezhnev Doctrine.

In late spring Bush spoke out on his hopes for East–West relations in a series of speeches and quietly approved the subsidized sale of 1,500,000 tons of wheat to the Soviets. In a Moscow meeting with Secretary Baker, Gorbachev not only endorsed the resumption of START, with the goal of deep cuts in strategic arsenals, but also stated that he would unilaterally withdraw 500 warheads from eastern Europe and accept NATO's request for asymmetrical reductions in conventional armaments. In response, Bush announced that the time had come "to move beyond containment" and to "seek the integration of the Soviet Union into the community of nations." Western European leaders were even more eager: Chancellor Kohl and Gorbachev agreed in June to support self-determination and arms reductions and to build a "common European home."

For Gorbachev the policies of glasnost, free elections, and warm relations with Western leaders were a calculated risk born of the Soviet Union's severe economic crisis and need for

Western help. For other Communist regimes, however, Moscow's "new thinking" was an unalloyed disaster. The governments of eastern Europe owed their existence to the myth of the "world proletarian revolution" and their survival to police-state controls backed by the threat of Soviet military power. Now, however, the Soviet leader himself had renounced the right of intervention, and he urged eastern European Communist parties to imitate perestroika and glasnost. Eastern European bosses like Erich Honecker of East Germany and Miloš Jakeš of Czechoslovakia quietly made common cause with hard-liners in Moscow.

Reaction to Protests in China and the Soviet Bloc

Meanwhile, a protest movement emerged in China in the spring of 1989, the suppression of which had an effect on the similar wave of democracy in the Soviet bloc. Ever since the late 1950s the Chinese Communist party had regularly and officially denounced the Soviets as revisionists—Marxist heretics—and Gorbachev's deeds and words only proved their rectitude. Even so, since the death of Mao Zedong the Chinese leadership had itself adopted limited reforms under the banner of the Four Modernizations and had permitted a modicum of highly successful free enterprise while retaining a monopoly of political power. When Hu Yaobang, a former leader, died on April 15, 1989, however, tens of thousands of students and other protesters began to gather in Chinese cities to demand democratic reforms. Within a week 100,000 people filled Tiananmen Square in Peking and refused to disperse despite strong warnings. The 70th anniversary of the May Fourth Movement, the first student movement in modern Chinese history, propelled the protests, as did Gorbachev's own arrival for

TIANANMEN SQUARE MASSACRE

Tens of thousands of students gathered in Tiananmen Square in Beijing, China, in the spring of 1989, demanding democratic, political, social, and economic reforms. The initial government response was to issue stern warnings but take no action against the mounting crowds in the square. Similar demonstrations rose up in a number of other Chinese cities, notably Shanghai, Nanjing, Xi'an, Changsha, and Chengdu. However, the principal outside media coverage was in Beijing, in part because a large number of Western journalists had gathered there to report on the visit to China by Soviet leader Mikhail Gorbachev in mid-May. Shortly after his arrival, a demonstration in Tiananmen Square drew some one million participants and was widely broadcast overseas.

Meanwhile, an intense debate ensued among government and party officials on how to handle the mounting protests. Moderates advocated negotiating with the demonstrators and offering concessions. However, they were overruled by hard-liners led by Chinese premier Li Peng and supported by paramount elder statesman Deng Xiaoping, who, fearing anarchy, insisted on forcibly suppressing the protests.

During the last two weeks of May, martial law was declared in Beijing, and army troops were stationed around the city. However, an attempt by the troops to reach Tiananmen Square was thwarted when Beijing citizens flooded the streets and blocked their way. Protesters remained in large numbers in Tiananmen Square, centring themselves around a plaster statue called "Goddess of Democracy," near the northern end of the square. Western journalists also maintained a presence there, often providing live coverage of the events.

By the beginning of June, the government was ready to act again. On the night of June 3–4, tanks and heavily armed troops advanced toward Tiananmen Square, opening fire on or crushing those who again tried to block their way. Once the soldiers reached the square, a number of the few thousand remaining demonstrators there chose to leave rather than face a continuation of the confrontation. By morning the area had been cleared of protesters, though sporadic shootings occurred throughout the day. The military also moved in forcibly against protesters in several other Chinese cities. By June 5 the military had secured complete control, though during the day there was a notable, widely reported incident involving a lone protester momentarily facing down a column of tanks as it advanced on him near the square.

In the aftermath of the crackdown, the United States instituted economic and diplomatic sanctions for a time, and many other foreign governments criticized China's handling of the protesters. The Western media quickly labeled the events of June 3–4 a "massacre." The Chinese government arrested thousands of suspected dissidents; many of them received prison sentences of varying lengths of time, and a number were executed. However, several dissident leaders managed to escape from China and sought refuge in the West.

From the outset of the incident, the Chinese government's official stance was to downplay its significance, labeling the protesters "counterrevolutionaries" and minimizing the extent of the military's actions on June 3–4. The government's count of those killed was 241 (including soldiers), with some 7,000 wounded; most other estimates have put the death toll much higher. In the years since the incident, the government generally has attempted to suppress references to it. Public commemoration of the incident is officially banned. However, the residents of Hong Kong have held an annual vigil on the anniversary of the crackdown, even after Hong Kong reverted to Chinese administration in 1997.

the first Sino-Soviet summit in 30 years. By May 20 the situation was completely out of control: more than 1,000,000 demonstrators occupied large sections of Peking, and on the 29th students erected a statue called the "Goddess of Democracy" in Tiananmen Square.

Behind the scenes a furious power struggle ensued between party chiefs advocating accommodation and those calling for the use of force; it remained uncertain whether the People's Liberation Army could be trusted to act against the demonstration. Finally, on June 3, military units from distant provinces were called in to move against the crowds; they did so efficiently, killing hundreds of protesters. Thousands more were arrested in the days that followed.

The suppression of the democratic movement in China conditioned the thinking of eastern European officials and protesters alike for months. Taking heart from Gorbachev's reformism, citizens hoped that the time had finally come when they might expand their narrow political options. They moved cautiously, however, not wholly trusting that the Soviet Union would stand aside and fearing that at any moment their local state security police would opt for a "Tiananmen solution." Nonetheless, in July, at the annual Warsaw Pact meeting, Gorbachev called on each member state to pursue "independent solutions [to] national problems" and said that there were "no universal models of Socialism." At the same time Bush toured Poland and Hungary, praising their steps toward democracy and offering aid, but saying and doing nothing that would embarrass the Soviets or take strategic advantage of their difficulties. So it was that for the first time both superpower leaders indicated with increasing clarity that they intended to stand aside and allow events in eastern Europe to take their course independent of Cold War considerations. Gorbachev had indeed repealed the Brezhnev Doctrine, and Bush had done nothing to impel him to reimpose it.

The results were almost immediate. In August a trickle, then a flood of would-be émigrés from East Germany tried the escape route open through Hungary to Austria and West Germany. In the same month the chairman of the Soviet

Central Committee admitted the existence of the secret proto-
cols in the German-Soviet Nonaggression Pact under which
Stalin had annexed Latvia, Lithuania, and Estonia. On the
50th anniversary of the pact, August 23, an estimated 1,000,000
Balts formed a human chain linking their capitals to denounce
the annexation as illegal and to demand self-determination. In
September the Hungarian government suspended its effort to
stave off the flight of East Germans, and by the end of the
month more than 30,000 had escaped to the West.
Demonstrations for democracy began in East Germany itself in
late September, spreading from Leipzig to Dresden and other
cities. On October 6–7 Gorbachev, visiting in honour of the
German Democratic Republic's 40th anniversary, urged East
Germany to adopt Soviet-style reforms and said that its policy
would be made in Berlin, not Moscow.

Against this background of massive and spreading popular
defiance of Communist regimes, Western governments maintained a prudent silence about the internal affairs of Soviet-bloc
states, while sending clear signals to Moscow of the potential
benefits of continued liberalization. When Gorbachev's neme-
sis Yeltsin visited the United States in September, the
administration kept a discreet distance. Later that month
Shevardnadze held extensive and private talks with Baker; he
dropped once and for all the Soviet demand that the American
SDI program be included in the START negotiations. In the
first week of October the European Community, West Germany,
and then (at the insistence of Congress) the United States
offered emergency aid totalling $2,000,000,000 to the democ-
ratizing Polish government. The chairman of the U.S. Federal
Reserve Board went to Moscow to advise the Soviets on how
they, too, might make the transition to a market economy, and
Secretary Baker proclaimed, "We want perestroika to succeed."
A month later Gorbachev gave the first indication of the limits

to reform, warning that Western efforts to "export capitalism" or "interfere with east European politics would be a great mistake." By that time, however, the collapse of Communism in the satellite states, at least, was irreversible.

The Satellite States Declare Independence

Hungary became the second (after Poland) to seize its independence when the National Assembly, on October 18, 1989, amended its constitution to abolish the Socialist party's "leading role" in society, legalize non-Communist political parties, and change the name of the country from the "People's Republic" to simply the "Republic of Hungary."

East Germany, one of the most repressive of all Soviet-bloc states, was next. By late October crowds numbering more than 300,000 rose up in Leipzig and Dresden to demand the ouster of the Communist regime. On November 1 the East German cabinet bowed before the unrelenting, nonviolent pressure of its people by reopening its border with Czechoslovakia. On November 3 the ministers in charge of security and the police resigned. The next day a reported 1,000,000 demonstrators jammed the streets of East Berlin to demand democracy, prompting the resignations of the rest of the cabinet.

After 50,000 more people had fled the country in the ensuing week, the East German government threw in the towel. On November 9 it announced that exit visas would be granted immediately to all citizens wishing to "visit the West" and that all border points were now open. At first, citizens did not dare believe—hundreds of East Germans had lost their lives trying to escape after the Berlin Wall went up in August 1961—but when some did, the news flowed like electricity that the Berlin

East Berliners celebrate the fall of the Berlin Wall on Nov. 11, 1989, two days after restrictions on leaving the country were lifted.

Wall had fallen. A week later the dreaded Stasis, or state security police, were disbanded. By December 1 the East German Volkskammer (parliament) renounced the Communist Socialist Unity Party's "leading role" in society and began to expose the corruption and brutality that had characterized the Honecker regime. A new coalition government took control and planned free national elections for May 1990.

Czechoslovaks were the fourth people to carry out a nonviolent revolution, though at first frustrated by the hard-line regime's continued will to repress. A demonstration on November 17 in Wenceslas Square in Prague was broken up by force. The Czechoslovaks, emboldened by events in East Germany and the absence of a Soviet reaction, turned out in ever larger numbers, however, demanding free elections and then cheering the rehabilitated hero of the 1968 Prague Spring, Alexander Dubček. The entire cabinet resigned, and the Communist Central Committee promised a special congress to discuss the party's future. The dissident liberal playwright Václav Havel denounced the shake-up as a trick, crowds of 800,000 turned out to demand democratic elections, and Czechoslovak workers declared a two-hour general strike as proof of their solidarity. The government caved in, abandoning the Communist party's "leading role" on November 29, opening the border with Austria on the 30th, and announcing a new coalition cabinet on December 8. President Gustav Husák resigned on the 10th and free elections were scheduled for the 28th. By the end of the year Havel was president of Czechoslovakia and Dubček was parliamentary chairman.

The fifth and sixth satellite peoples to break out of the 45-year Communist lockstep were the Bulgarians and Romanians. The former had an easy time of it after the Communist party secretary and president, Todor Zhivkov, resigned on November 10. Within a month crowds in Sofia called for democratization, and the Central Committee leader voluntarily surrendered the party's "leading role." Romania, however, suffered a bloodbath. There the Communist dictator Nicolae Ceaușescu had built a ferocious personal tyranny defended by ubiquitous and brutal security forces. He intended to ride out the anti-Communist wave in eastern Europe and preserve his rule. Thus, when crowds of Romanian citizens demonstrated for democracy in imitation of events elsewhere, the government denounced them as "Fascist reactionaries" and ordered its security forces to shoot to kill. Courageous crowds continued to rally and regular army units joined the rebellion, and, when the Soviets indicated their opposition to Ceaușescu, civil war broke out. On December 22 popular forces captured Ceaușescu while he attempted to flee, tried him on several charges, including genocide, and executed him on the 25th. An interim National Salvation Front Council took over and announced elections for May 1990. By the end of the year the Czechoslovaks and Hungarians had already concluded agreements with Moscow providing for the rapid withdrawal of Soviet military forces from their countries.

Aftermath of the Breakup

In the span of just three months the unthinkable had happened: all of eastern Europe had broken free of Communist domination and won the right to resume the independent national existences that Nazi aggression had extinguished beginning in 1938. The force of popular revulsion against the Stalinist regimes imposed after World War II was the cause of the explosion, and advanced communications technology permitted the news to spread quickly, triggering revolts in one capital after another. What enabled the popular forces to express themselves, and succeed, however, was singular and simple: the abrogation of the Brezhnev Doctrine by Mikhail Gorbachev. Once it became known that the Red Army would not intervene to crush dissent, as it had in all previous crises, the whole Stalinist empire was revealed as a sham and flimsy structure. For decades, Western apologists for the Soviet bloc had argued that eastern European Socialism was somehow indigenous, even that the East Germans had developed a "separate nationality," and that the Soviets had a legitimate security interest in eastern Europe. Gorbachev himself proved them wrong when he let eastern Europe go free in 1989.

What were his motives for doing so? Certainly the Soviet army and the KGB must have watched in horror as their empire, purchased at terrific cost in World War II, simply disintegrated. Perhaps Gorbachev calculated, in line with the "new thinking," that the U.S.S.R. did not need eastern Europe to ensure its own security and that maintaining the empire was no longer worth the financial and political cost. At a time when the Soviet Union was in severe economic crisis and needed Western help more than ever, jettisoning eastern Europe would unburden his budget and do more than anything to attract Western good-will. Nevertheless, it is hard to believe that Gorbachev ever intended things to work out as they did. It is far more likely that he intended merely to throw his support to progressive Communists eager to implement perestroika in their own countries and thereby strengthen his own position vis-à-vis the hard-liners in the Soviet party. His ploy, however, had three attendant risks: first, that popular revolt might go so far as to dismantle Communism and the Warsaw Pact altogether; second, that the eastern European revolution might spread to nationalities within the U.S.S.R. itself; and third, that the NATO powers might try to exploit eastern European unrest to its own strategic advantage. The first fear quickly came true, and as 1989 came to an end, Gorbachev's foreign and domestic policies were increasingly directed toward forestalling the second and third dangers.

Concerning possible Western exploitation of the retreat of Communism, Shevardnadze expressed as early as October the Soviet Union's desire to pursue the dissolution of the Warsaw Pact and NATO military alliances. (Of course, the Warsaw Pact was in the course of dissolving from within.) Then, in November, Gorbachev warned against Western attempts to export capital-ism. Western European leaders were anxious to reassure him, as was President Bush at the December 2–3 Malta summit. Only

A pro-independence demonstration in Vilnius, Lithuania, on Jan. 10, 1990.

a few days before, however, Chancellor Kohl had alerted the Soviets and the world that he intended to press forward at once on the most difficult problem of all arising from the liberation of eastern Europe: the reunification of Germany. That prospect, and the conditions under which it might occur, would dominate Great Power diplomacy in 1990.

Gorbachev had every reason to fear that his second nightmare would come true: the spillover of popular revolt into the Soviet Union itself. The first of the subject nationalities of the U.S.S.R. to demand self-determination were the Lithuanians, whose Communist Party Congress voted by a huge majority to declare its independence from the party's leadership in Moscow and to move toward an independent, democratic state. Gorbachev denounced the move at once and warned of bloodshed if the Lithuanians persisted. In January 1990 his personal visit to the Lithuanian capital, Vilnius, to calm the waters provoked a rally of 250,000 people demanding the abrogation of the Soviets' "illegal" 1940 annexation. When in that same month Soviet troops entered the Azerbaijan capital, Baku, and killed more than 50 Azerbaijani nationalists, fears arose that the Baltic states might suffer the same fate. Gorbachev let it be known that, the liberation of eastern Europe notwithstanding, he would not preside over the dissolution of the U.S.S.R.

The Reunification of Germany

Even before they had succeeded in chasing the Communists out of their government, East Germans had already begun to "unify" the country with their feet: 133,000 people picked up and moved westward in the month after the fall of the Berlin Wall. Such an influx of people placed tremendous strains on West Germany and all but forced Chancellor Kohl to begin immediate measures toward reunification in order to stem the tide. On November 28, 1989, he shocked the world with his announcement of a 10-point plan under which the East and West German governments would gradually expand their cooperation on specific issues until full economic, then political unity was achieved. He proposed no timetable and sought to appease the Soviets and western European powers alike by emphasizing that the process must occur within the contexts of the Conference on Security and Co-operation in Europe (CSCE; now the Organization for Security and Co-operation in Europe), the European Community, and East–West disarmament regimes.

The Kohl plan was more than an emergency response, however; it was also the culmination of a West German policy dating back to the founding of the two Germanies in 1949. Reunification was provided for in the West German Basic Law (constitution) and had remained the primary goal, no matter how distant, of its foreign policy. Even Willy Brandt's *Ostpolitik* in 1969 had differed only in regard to means, looking to increased contacts and aid to educate East Germans about the freedom and prosperity prevailing in the West, and so gradually and peacefully to undermine the legitimacy of the East German regime.

APPREHENSION AMONG THE GREAT POWERS

Almost no one was entirely comfortable with the prospect of a reunited Germany. West Germany alone had become the economic colossus of Europe; augmented by the East, it might come to dominate the European Community. Moreover, how was a united Germany to be prevented from aspiring to military power or hegemony in the power vacuum of eastern Europe? The Soviets seemed unlikely to countenance a united Germany fully allied with the United States and the EC, while a neutral Germany might become a loose cannon vacillating between Moscow and the West. So it was that on the day after the Malta summit, President Bush declared his support for a gradually reunited Germany to remain in NATO and the EC, within a "Europe whole and free." French President Mitterrand warned the Germans against pushing it too hard, while British Prime Minister Thatcher was openly skeptical. Gorbachev was expected to demand large concessions in return for his approval. Bush presumably had reassured him at Malta that events would not be allowed to get out of control. To underscore their intention to assert their rights in Germany dating back to the 1945 Potsdam conference, the Soviets requested a meeting of the old Allied Control Council in Berlin. To underscore their intention to respect Soviet feelings, the other World War II Allied powers (the United States, Great Britain, and France) agreed to meet on December 11.

The reunification of Germany for so long had been thought impossible and, by many (perhaps most) people in the U.S.S.R., France, Britain, and the United States, even undesirable. Now, suddenly it appeared inevitable. Whatever their misgivings, the Allies could hardly deny Germany the right to the self-determination they claimed for themselves and all other peoples. When members of NATO and the Warsaw Pact convened at Ottawa, on February 11, 1990, Bush skillfully won universal agreement to a prudent format for talks on the unification of Germany. The French, British, and Soviets had considered involving the four powers from the start in group negotiations with the Germans, thereby calling into question German sovereignty. Bush's plan, however, would permit the German states themselves to work out their future and then submit their wishes to the four powers for final approval. These "two plus four" talks were expected to be a slow, deliberative process.

NEGOTIATIONS AND TERMS

In fact, the overwhelming will of the German people and the press of events brought negotiations quickly to a head. First, the East German elections on March 18 revealed a strong majority in favour of immediate unification. Second, the East German economy underwent sudden collapse after the disappearance of Communist discipline and the flight of hundreds of thousands of people. Third, the East German infrastructure was now revealed as decrepit and backward, the environment grossly polluted, and the currency worthless. Talks began at once on an emergency unification of the two Germanies' economies, and in April, after much hand-wringing, Kohl and the

Deutsche Bundesbank accepted a plan to replace the East German currency with deutsche marks on a one-to-one basis. The "two plus four" talks moved to the foreign ministerial level in May, and within two weeks East and West Germany published their terms for their imminent merger. Moreover, it would not be achieved by the laborious crafting of a new constitution but by the quicker provisions of Article 23 of the West German Basic Law, whereby new provinces could adhere to the existing constitution by a simple majority vote. The Bundestag (parliament) approved these terms on June 21, and West and East Germany were unified economically on July 1.

Assurances were required to the effect that a united Germany, far from making NATO more threatening, would in fact be constrained by its membership in the U.S.-led alliance; that German military power would be limited by treaty and that Soviet troops might remain in East Germany for a time as a guarantee; that Soviet–German relations would improve after unification and yield vital economic assistance for the Soviet Union; and that the new Germany would recognize and respect existing international boundaries. Bush moved to satisfy the first and second of these desiderata at the NATO summit in July; its declaration defined NATO and the Warsaw Pact as no longer enemies, renounced NATO's long-standing policy on first use of nuclear weapons, agreed to limits (proposed by Shevardnadze) on the size of the German army, and invited the Warsaw Pact countries to establish "regular diplomatic liaison with NATO."

The third desideratum—improved Soviet–German relations—was, of course, up to Chancellor Kohl to satisfy. He offered to cut the German army to 370,000 men, renounce chemical, biological, and nuclear weapons, and aid in financing Soviet troops during an eventual withdrawal over a three-to-four-year transition period. He also extended $5,000,000,000 in credits, with an expectation of more to follow. In return he secured Gorbachev's acceptance of a united, sovereign, democratic German state to remain a full member of the Western alliance and the EC. Kohl also took pains to reassure the French that the new united Germany would pose no threat. In the ongoing EC deliberations about the greater unification to take effect in 1992, Kohl sided constantly and strongly with the French position. He made it as clear as possible that the Germans were "good Europeans" and that their unity would occur harmlessly within the context of greater European and Atlantic communities.

Meanwhile, the bilateral talks between East and West Germans proceeded at an emergency pace. The two governments signed the terms for their political union on August 31. The four Allied powers then ratified them in their own Final Settlement with Respect to Germany. Those signatures, affixed in Moscow on September 12, formally brought World War II to an end. The next day Germany and the U.S.S.R. signed a treaty of 20 years' duration pledging to each other friendly relations and recognition of borders and renouncing the use of force. The four Allied powers renounced their rights in Germany on October 1, the final settlement took effect on October 3, 1990, and Germans tearfully celebrated their reunification.

One final issue remained—that of Germany's permanent boundaries. Western powers and especially the Polish government had pressured Kohl from the beginning to recognize for all time the inviolability of the Oder–Neisse border and thus the permanent loss to Germany of Silesia, eastern Pomerania, Danzig (Gdańsk), and East Prussia. At first Kohl hung back, earning for himself much abuse from Western statesmen and scaremongers. His tactic seems to have been to make a show of standing up for Germany's lost territories in the east in order to send a message to the Polish government about the need to respect the rights of ethnic Germans in Poland, as well as to minimize the appeal of the right-wing Republikaner party to the German electorate. As soon as German unity was assured, Kohl accepted Germany's boundaries as permanent, and he signed a treaty to that effect with Poland on November 14.

Five days later the second CSCE summit convened in Paris to proclaim the end of the Cold War. In the Conventional Forces in Europe Treaty, the NATO and Soviet sides each pledged to limit themselves to 20,000 battle tanks and 20,000 artillery tubes, 6,800 combat aircraft, 30,000 other armoured combat vehicles, and 2,000 attack helicopters. The CSCE member states signed the Charter of Paris for a New Europe, in which the Soviets, Americans, and Europeans both east and west announced to the world that Europe was henceforth united, that all blocs—military and economic—had ceased to exist, and that all member states stood for democracy, freedom, and human rights.

Why the Soviet Retreat?

On October 15, 1990, Mikhail Gorbachev travelled to Stockholm to receive the Nobel Prize for Peace in honour of his having done much to bring the Cold War to a close. While few people in Europe and North America denied that Gorbachev's restraint in 1989 was largely responsible for the liberation of eastern Europe or criticized the directions of his reforms in the Soviet Union, the Nobel Prize seemed to imply standards of historical and moral judgment that struck many critics as, at best, strange. Was the Soviet president to be credited with the world's most prestigious prize for not sending in tank columns to crush innocent and unarmed people in foreign countries? What about the eastern European peoples themselves, who bravely seized their freedom in spite of the risks? Or the Western leaders whose denunciations of the

Soviet empire encouraged the Polish Solidarity movement and other eastern European resisters?

Indeed, as soon as people in the West caught their breath after the cascade of events in 1989–90, they began to argue over why the Cold War had ended, why it ended when it did, and to whom the credit should go. Academic and liberal opinion favoured theories crediting Gorbachev and the generation of "new thinkers" in the Soviet Union for the transformations. Conservatives preferred to give the credit to the statesmen of containment who had stood up to Soviet pressure for 40 years. (When President Bush visited Poland upon the invitation of Lech Wałęsa in 1989, thousands of Poles lined the streets to cheer and wave banners reading "Thank you!")

Historians have argued over the end of the Cold War as intensely as they argued over its beginning, but some general observations can be made. First, the Cold War ended because the special sources of conflict and distrust between the Soviet Union and the West disappeared in 1989. That is not to say that geopolitical rivalry disappeared, or that conflicts of interest would not recur in many parts of the world. Great Power politics would go on. At the same time, the liberation of eastern Europe, unification of Germany, reduction of armaments, and suspension of Leninist ideological war against the outer world were symptomatic of the changed nature of superpower relations. Second, those relations changed their nature over the years 1985–90 because the Soviet leadership lost the ability or the will, or both, to prosecute the Cold War and seemingly came to realize that even the gains they had made in the Cold War were not in the best interests of the Soviet Union. Rather, the U.S.S.R. and its satellites and client states constituted a network of obligations that seriously strained the resources of the central economy and that had called into being a hostile alliance consisting of all the other major industrial powers of the world: the United States, Britain, France, West Germany, Japan, and China. What was more, the Communist (or Stalinist) command structure had proved woefully inadequate to the demands of a technological age.

In sum, the Soviet Union had embarked under Stalin on a Sisyphean struggle against the entire outer world, only to discover over time that its huge conventional army was of doubtful utility, its nuclear arsenal unusable, its diplomatic attempts to divide the enemy alliance unsuccessful, its Third World clients expensive and of dubious value, and its pervasive apparatus for espionage, disinformation, terror, and demoralization of temporary effect only. Always the Western peoples recovered their will and dynamism; always the Soviet Union fell further behind, until finally, after 40 years, the empire fell, exhausted, to the ground.

That was when the younger generation came to the fore, promoting the "new thinking" that had sprung up from disgust with the rigid and brutal structures dating from Stalin and the rigid and counterproductive policies dating from Brezhnev. Perhaps Gorbachev himself remained a committed Marxist-Leninist—he said so at every opportunity—but the practical effect of his repudiation of old structures and policies was to dismantle much that had provoked the fear and hostility of the West in the first place. Nor would releasing eastern Europe suffice to reverse the inevitable decline of the Communist empire. The age of microelectronics, computers, space technology, and global communications was also an age in which human creativity, not brute labour, was the most valuable asset in a nation's economic and military strength. Far from unleashing creativity and spontaneous production, as Marxist theory predicted, Soviet Communism had stifled it—through terror, bureaucratization, the lack of a profit motive and market mechanism, and hierarchical, centralized decision making.

Eventually, if the Soviet Union were to remain even a great power, much less a superpower, it would have to jettison not only its subject empire but also Communism itself.

George Kennan predicted in his famous "Long Telegram" of 1946 and "X" article of 1947 that the Soviets would ultimately fail to digest the empire they had swallowed and would have to disgorge it. In the meantime, the West had to contain Soviet influence, neither retreating into isolationism nor overreacting militarily, and above all remaining confident about its basic human values. He was right. The most fundamental, long-range reason for the end of the Cold War was that Communism was based on profound contradictions and a misreading of human nature. So long as other nations refused to surrender to their fear, the Soviet system could never prevail. Perhaps the exhortations and policies of Reagan and Thatcher did determine the timing of the Soviet collapse, but the collapse was bound to come sooner or later.

Students of Soviet history with a more sociological bent offered yet another explanation for the Gorbachev phenomenon, based on irrepressible trends within Soviet society itself. For whatever horrors he committed against his own people, Stalin had made the U.S.S.R. into a modern, industrial, and primarily urban country. Khrushchev introduced television and spaceflight, and Brezhnev, through détente, multiplied the foreign contacts and experience of Soviet citizens. By the late 1970s a great percentage of Soviet people had ceased to be illiterate peasants easily suppressed, propagandized, and drafted into massive military, agricultural, or construction projects. Instead, a second- or third-generation urban population had grown up that inevitably came to demand more access to the information, political influence, and material rewards available to people of their station in the West. Once glasnost gave them a voice, these new "middle classes" loudly expressed their dissatisfaction with a regime that had become not only inhumane but irrational, even on its own materialistic terms. According to this view, therefore, Sovietism was doomed even by its relative success: the more modern the U.S.S.R. became, the less legitimate its party dictatorship became in the eyes of its educated classes.

A final, long-range interpretation laid stress on the nationality crisis in eastern Europe and the Soviet Union. The U.S.S.R. was the world's last great multinational empire. The Communist party maintained its tight control over the Balts, Ukrainians, Moldavians, Georgians, Uzbeks, Armenians, and a dozen other major peoples by a combination of economic controls, censorship and propaganda, police methods, suppression of national cultures and churches, Russification, dispersal of populations, and in the last resort, force—all justified by the myth that Marxism transcended "bourgeois" nationalism and ensured equality and prosperity to all. Glasnost, however, released the real and abiding national sentiments of all the peoples under the Soviet yoke, allowing them to organize and agitate, while the economic breakdown gave the lie to Soviet promises. Finally, the discrediting of Communism itself removed the last justification for the very existence of the empire. Gorbachev did not foresee how far his policy of limited free expression would get out of hand, and by the time he did it was too late. He then gave up trying to hold eastern Europe and concentrated instead on trying to hold the U.S.S.R. together.

The Collapse of the Soviet Union

The failure of Gorbachev's economic reforms continued, with the Soviet GNP falling even further in 1989–90. Shortages grew worse, and even the old Soviet command structure broke down as the constituent republics, one by one, set up their own economic systems and voted to subordinate the laws of the Soviet Union to local laws. Boris Yeltsin, the Russian leader, resigned from the Communist party and became the acknowledged leader of democratic forces throughout the U.S.S.R. Separatism spread among the republics, with the Baltic states taking the lead in hopes of winning complete independence. At the same time, hard-liners in the KGB, the army, and the Communist party gradually regrouped after the buffetings of previous years and criticized Gorbachev for being too soft on dissent. The middle ground of moderate reformism was disappearing from beneath Gorbachev's feet. Late in 1990 he began to issue sterner warnings to Yeltsin to cease and desist, and he insisted that the Baltics and other republics submit to his newly drafted union treaty regulating the relationship between them and the Soviet central government. He also won still greater emergency powers for himself as president from the Congress of People's Deputies.

The first hint that the Soviets might crack down on dissident Soviet ethnic groups was the resignation of Shevardnadze in December 1990. The next month, the Western powers initiated a war against Saddam Hussein's regime in Iraq, in protest of Iraq's invasion of Kuwait. With the West distracted, Soviet security forces entered Vilnius, the capital of Lithuania, which had declared independence on March 11, 1990. Several people were killed in the ensuing bloodshed between Lithuanian patriots and the Soviet troops.

Within weeks, hundreds of thousands of Muscovites defied the ban on public demonstrations, six Soviet republics boycotted a referendum on Gorbachev's new union plan, and Ukrainian coal miners went on strike. When Yeltsin was elected president of the Russian republic with 60 percent of the vote on June 12, he clearly emerged as a more legitimate apostle of reform. Western governments observed these challenges to Soviet authority with a mixture of delight and dismay. American conservatives urged the White House to support the republics' struggle for freedom, but Bush insisted on caution. He had worked closely with Gorbachev to end the Cold War peaceably and feared that his fall from power would mean either the return of Communist hard-liners or the crack-up of the U.S.S.R. into quarreling regions. Moreover, given his lack of experience and reputation as a hard-drinking, impulsive populist, Yeltsin seemed suspect. In what proved to be a final bid to help Gorbachev, Bush flew to Moscow on July 29 to sign the START treaty for reduc-tion of nuclear arsenals, then delivered a speech, later mocked as his "Chicken Kiev" speech, in which he warned the Ukrainian parliament against "suicidal nationalism."

Gorbachev's fate was sealed, however, on August 19 when a so-called Emergency Committee of Soviet hard-liners removed him from office while he was vacationing in Crimea and imposed martial law. The task of resistance fell to Yeltsin, who branded the coup leaders as traitors, barricaded himself inside the Russian parliament surrounded by his supporters, and dared the military to attack their fellow citizens. After one brief clash, the soldiers indeed wavered and the coup collapsed within 48 hours. Gorbachev was returned to the office of Soviet president but never regained real power, which had clearly passed to the courageous Yeltsin. Moreover, the failed coup destroyed the last remnants of fear or loyalty that had held the Soviet empire together. Estonia and Latvia joined Lithuania by declaring independence, and this time the United States immediately extended recognition. On August 24 Ukraine declared independence, Belorussia (Belarus) the next day, and Moldavia (Moldova) on the 27th. The Russian parliament, in turn, granted Yeltsin sweeping emergency powers to liberal-ize the economy and suppress the Communist party. Even then Gorbachev tried to salvage some sort of economic and security

① RUSSIA	⑤ BELARUS	⑨ ARMENIA	⑬ TURKMENISTAN
② ESTONIA	⑥ UKRAINE	⑩ AZERBAIJAN	⑭ KYRGYZSTAN
③ LATVIA	⑦ MOLDOVA	⑪ KAZAKHSTAN	⑮ TAJIKISTAN
④ LITHUANIA	⑧ GEORGIA	⑫ UZBEKISTAN	

The Cold War effectively came to an end when the Soviet Union formally dissolved on December 8, 1991, having splintered into 15 separate states.

union, but he gave up on December 1 when Ukrainian voters approved independence in a referendum.

On the 8th Yeltsin and the newly elected presidents of Ukraine and Belarus declared that the U.S.S.R. had ceased to exist and replaced it with the loose Commonwealth of Independent States. The U.S. ambassador, Robert Strauss, finally acknowledged that Gorbachev was "in decline" and that henceforth Yeltsin's government "are the people with whom we'll deal." Gorbachev resigned on December 25, the hammer-and-sickle flag was lowered from the Kremlin, and in its place rose the white, blue, and red flag of Russia. It assumed the U.S.S.R.'s seat on the UN Security Council, and all Soviet embassies became Russian embassies.

The dissolution of the Soviet Union completed the liquidation of the Cold War by extinguishing Leninism in its homeland. Happily, the chaos feared by the Bush administration did not erupt, but the emergence of 15 independent states from the wreckage posed a plethora of new problems. All the states were in economic distress as they began to make the transition from centrally planned to market economies. All contained significant national minorities; none had secure, legitimate boundaries; and Russia, Ukraine, and Kazakhstan possessed sizable stocks of nuclear weapons. Thus, the world might be less scary in the short run, but it did not promise to be more stable.

Conclusion

Within one week's time, in the summer of 1991, the 74-year-old Soviet Union ceased to exist. The Soviet Union had been the world's largest country. At its greatest extent, it covered an area of 8.6 million square miles (22.4 million square kilometers), almost seven times the area of India and two and a half times that of the United States. It encompassed one-sixth of Earth's landmass, including half of Europe and about two-fifths of Asia. The population of the country in 1991 was more than 290 million, and the future of all those peoples was uncertain.

Whatever the legal position, the union republics had begun to act as if they were sovereign states and were negotiating with each other, bypassing the vestigial central government. This process culminated on Dec. 8, 1991, in the signing of an agreement between the three Slavic republics of Russia, Ukraine, and Belarus for the establishment of the Commonwealth of Independent States (CIS), with an agreed common policy for foreign affairs and defense. The CIS later came to include all the remaining republics except the Baltic states of Estonia, Latvia, and Lithuania: Armenia, Azerbaijan, Belorussia (now Belarus), Georgia (which withdrew from the CIS in 2009), Kazakhstan, Kirghizia (now Kyrgyzstan), Moldavia (now Moldova), Russia, Tajikistan, Turkmenistan, Ukraine, and Uzbekistan. However, great difficulty was experienced in arriving at agreed-upon policies. The future thus remained uncertain, but there could be no disagreement with the statement by the leaders of the Commonwealth that "the U.S.S.R. has ceased to exist as a geopolitical reality."

Even before the Soviet Union's official breakup, the world had faced its first post–Cold War crisis—Iraq's invasion of Kuwait and the subsequent Persian Gulf War, conducted by a UN coalition led by the United States. It was the first significant conflict since 1945 in which the interests of the United States and Soviet Union were not in direct opposition. Though Iraq was quickly defeated, ongoing and new crises around the world, from Israel and Palestine to Yugoslavia and North Korea, proved that diplomacy in the 1990s and beyond would be just as fraught as it had been during the Cold War.

Glossary

abrogation Formal repeal of an act.

concurrent Operating or occurring at the same time.

containment The policy or the process of preventing the expansion beyond prescribed limits of a hostile power or ideology, especially by employing political, economic, and propaganda pressure and by strengthening friendly powers; strategic foreign policy pursued by the United States in the late 1940s and the early 1950s in order to check the expansionist policy of the Soviet Union.

cordon sanitaire A chain of buffer states intended to provide protection against a country considered potentially aggressive or ideologically dangerous.

coup d'état The sudden, violent overthrow of an existing government by a small group.

denouement The ultimate outcome or result of any complex situation or sequence of events.

détente A slackening or relaxing, especially an easing or relaxation of strained relations and political tensions between nations; period of the easing of Cold War tensions between the U.S and the Soviet Union from 1967 to 1979.

domino theory The theory that if one country becomes Communist-controlled its neighboring countries will also succumb to Communist control.

exhortation Language intended to incite and encourage.

glasnost A policy introduced in the Soviet Union in the 1980s permitting open discussion of political and social issues and freer dissemination of news and information.

hegemony Dominant influence or authority, as of a government or state.

Ostpolitik "Eastern policy"; West German foreign policy begun in the late 1960s that was grounded in détente with Soviet-bloc countries, recognizing the East German government and expanding commercial relations with other Soviet-bloc countries.

perestroika Extensive restructuring and reform intended to revitalize the government and economy of the Soviet Union.

preemptive Marked by the seizing of the initiative, especially being or relating to a first military strike made to gain an advantage when a strike by the enemy is believed imminent.

promulgate To make known by open declaration; to put a new law into effect.

propound To offer for consideration, deliberation, or debate; put for solution; set forth.

proxy A person or state authorized to act for another.

quagmire A complex or precarious position where disengagement is difficult.

repudiation The act of refusing to be bound by the terms of a contract, treaty, or doctrine.

revisionism Advocacy of revision of an original doctrine or historical analysis; a movement among socialists to modify Marxian socialism especially so as to be evolutionary rather than revolutionary in spirit.

rimland A region on the periphery of the heartland.

scuttle To sink or attempt to sink by making holes through the bottom of; to damage severely or destroy completely; to sabotage.

Sisyphean Of, relating to, or suggestive of the labors of Sisyphus; specifically, requiring continual and often ineffective effort.

unmitigated Not made less severe or intense; unrelieved.

Bibliography

Origins of the Cold War

The Stalin–Truman years are documented by Harry S. Truman, *Memoirs*, 2 vol. (1955–56, reprinted 1986–87); Dean Acheson, *Present at the Creation: My Years in the State Department* (1969, reprinted 1987); George F. Kennan, *Memoirs*, 2 vol. (1967–72); and Dwight D. Eisenhower, *The White House Years*, 2 vol. (1963–65). Insightful histories include John Lewis Gaddis, *The United States and the Origins of the Cold War, 1941–1947* (1972), and *The Long Peace: Inquiries into the History of the Cold War* (1987); Paul Seabury, *The Rise and Decline of the Cold War* (1967); Louis J. Halle, *The Cold War as History* (1967, reprinted 1971); Daniel Yergin, *Shattered Peace: The Origins of the Cold War and the National Security State* (1977); Hugh Thomas, *Armed Truce: The Beginnings of the Cold War, 1945–46* (1986); and Melvyn P. Leffler, *A Preponderance of Power: National Security, the Truman Administration, and the Cold War* (1992).

The following are works of scholarship on the Cold War by authors who clearly regarded themselves as left-revision-ist: William Appleman Williams, *The Tragedy of American Diplomacy*, 2nd rev. ed. (1972); Gabriel Kolko, *The Roots of American Foreign Policy: An Analysis of Power and Purpose* (1969); Gar Alperovitz, *Atomic Diplomacy: Hiroshima and Potsdam: The Use of the Atomic Bomb and the American Confrontation with Soviet Power*, rev. ed. (1985); and David Horowitz, *The Free World Colossus: A Critique of American Foreign Policy in the Cold War*, rev. ed. (1971). However, Robert

J. Maddox, *The New Left and the Origins of the Cold War* (1973), critiques their logic and use of evidence.

The Soviet side is discussed in Vojtech Mastny, *Russia's Road to the Cold War: Diplomacy, Warfare, and the Politics of Communism, 1941–1945* (1979); Adam B. Ulam, *The Rivals: America and Russia Since World War II* (1971, reprinted 1983); David Holloway, *The Soviet Union and the Arms Race* (1983); and Thomas W. Wolfe, *Soviet Power and Europe, 1945–1970* (1970). Marshall D. Shulman, *Stalin's Foreign Policy Reappraised* (1963, reissued 1985); and William Taubman, *Stalin's American Policy: From Entente to Detente to Cold War* (1982), are sympathetic accounts. On the "wise men" surrounding Truman during the late 1940s, the critique by Lloyd C. Gardner, *Architects of Illusion: Men and Ideas in American Foreign Policy, 1941–1949* (1970), is useful; as is a later, more sympathetic work, Walter Isaacson and Evan Thomas, *The Wise Men: Six Friends and the World They Made: Acheson, Bohlen, Harriman, Kennan, Lovett, McCloy* (1986). The standard earlier work on atomic policy is *A History of the United States Atomic Energy Commission*, vol. 1 by Richard G. Hewlett and Oscar E. Anderson, *The New World, 1939/46* (1962), and vol. 2 by Richard G. Hewlett and Francis Duncan, *Atomic Shield, 1947/1952* (1969). A later work by Gregg Herken, *The Winning Weapon: The Atomic Bomb in the Cold War, 1945–1950* (1980), makes use of declassified material. Nuclear strategy is examined in the works by Marc Trachtenberg (ed.), *The Development of American Strategic Thought, 1945–1969*, 4 vol. in 6 (1987–88); and by Robert A. Divine, *Blowing on the Wind: The Nuclear Test Ban Debate, 1954–1960* (1978). The origins of the Korean War are explored in Bruce Cumings (ed.), *Child of Conflict: The Korean-American Relationship, 1943–1953* (1983); while the war itself is treated in the earlier study by David Rees, *Korea: The Limited War* (1964).

"Total" Cold War, 1957–72

The concept of "total Cold War" is described in Walter A. McDougall, *The Heavens and the Earth: A Political History of the Space Age* (1985). World trends after Sputnik are also the subject of W.W. Rostow, *The Diffusion of Power: An Essay in Recent History* (1972). The crises of the era are brilliantly analyzed in Marc Trachtenberg, *History and Strategy* (1991). Interesting memoirs are those by Nikita Khrushchev, *Khrushchev Remembers*, trans. from Russian (1970), and *Khrushchev Remembers: The Last Testament*, trans. from Russian (1974); Richard M. Nixon, *RN: The Memoirs of Richard Nixon* (1978); and Henry Kissinger, *White House Years* (1979). The Kennedy administration is considered in Arthur M. Schlesinger, Jr., *A Thousand Days: John F. Kennedy in the White House* (1965, reprinted 1983); Roger Hilsman, *To Move a Nation: The Politics of Foreign Policy in the Administration of John F. Kennedy* (1967); Graham T. Allison, *Essence of Decision: Explaining the Cuban Missile Crisis* (1971); Glenn T. Seaborg, *Kennedy, Khrushchev, and the Test Ban* (1981); and Desmond Ball, *Politics and Force Levels: The Strategic Missile Program of the Kennedy Administration* (1980). The Sino-Soviet split is explored by Alfred D. Low, *The Sino-Soviet Dispute: An Analysis of the Polemics* (1976), continued in his *Sino-Soviet Confrontation Since Mao Zedong: Dispute, Detente, or Conflict?* (1987); Donald S. Zagoria, *The Sino-Soviet Conflict, 1956–1961* (1962, reissued 1969); and William E. Griffith, *The Sino-Soviet Rift* (1964). The phenomenon of Gaullism is treated in Charles de Gaulle, *Memoirs of Hope: Renewal and Endeavor* (1971; originally published in French, 1970); W.W. Kulski, *De Gaulle and the World: The Foreign Policy of the Fifth French Republic* (1966); and Wilfrid L. Kohl, *French Nuclear Diplomacy* (1971).

Studies of postwar German policies include William E. Griffith, *The Ostpolitik of the Federal Republic of Germany* (1978); Gerhard Wettig, *Community and Conflict in the Socialist Camp: The Soviet Union, East Germany, and the German Problem, 1965–1972* (1975; originally published in German, 3 vol. in 4, 1972–73); and Peter H. Merkl, *German Foreign Policies, West & East: On the Threshold of a New European Era* (1974).

Third World Countries

General works on European decolonization include John D. Hargreaves, *The End of Colonial Rule in West Africa: Essays in Contemporary History* (1979); Prosser Gifford and W. Roger Lewis (eds.), *The Transfer of Power in Africa: Decolonization, 1940–1960* (1982); and Ann Williams, *Britain and France in the Middle East and North Africa, 1914–1967* (1968). Soviet penetration of the Third World is investigated in Robert C. Horn, *Soviet-Indian Relations: Issues and Influence* (1982); Christopher Stevens, *The Soviet Union and Black Africa* (1976); and Robert H. Donaldson (ed.), *The Soviet Union in the Third World: Successes and Failures* (1981). The Vietnam War is treated in William S. Turley, *The Second Indochina War: A Short Political and Military History, 1954–1975* (1986); Stanley Karnow, *Vietnam: A History* (1983); and George C. Herring, *America's Longest War: The United States and Vietnam, 1950–1975*, 2nd ed. (1986). Special topics are addressed in David Halberstam, *The Best and the Brightest* (1972, reprinted 1983), on U.S. involvement; on the Tet Offensive, Peter Braestrup, *Big Story: How the American Press and Television Reported and Interpreted the Crisis of Tet 1968 in Vietnam and Washington*, 2 vol. (1977); and on American military mistakes, Harry G. Summers, Jr., *On Strategy: A Critical Analysis of the Vietnam War* (1982).

The Global Village Since 1972

For the contemporary period, memoirs become increasingly important. All the principals in the Carter administration produced lengthy accounts: Jimmy Carter, *Keeping Faith: Memoirs of a President* (1982); Cyrus Vance, *Hard Choices: Critical Years in America's Foreign Policy* (1983); and Zbigniew Brzezinski, *Power and Principle: Memoirs of the National Security Adviser, 1977–1981* (1983). A fine summary of the administration is Gaddis Smith, *Morality, Reason, and Power: American Diplomacy in the Carter Years* (1986). China since 1970 is the subject of Roy Medvedev, *China and the Superpowers*, trans. from Russian (1986); and C.G. Jacobsen, *Sino-Soviet Relations Since Mao: The Chairman's Legacy* (1981). Middle Eastern diplomacy is expertly analyzed in Bahgat Korany and Ali E. Hillal Dessouki, *The Foreign Policies of Arab States* (1984); and general Third World problems in Stephen D. Krasner, *Structural Conflict: The Third World Against Global Liberalism* (1985). Soviet policy is the subject of Adam B. Ulam, *Dangerous Relations: The Soviet Union in World Politics, 1970–1982* (1983); Richard F. Staar, *USSR Foreign Policies After Detente*, rev. ed. (1987); and Roberta Goren, *The Soviet Union and Terrorism* (1984). A thorough account of the decline of détente between the United States and the U.S.S.R. is given in Raymond L. Garthoff, *Détente and Confrontation: American–Soviet Relations from Nixon to Reagan* (1985).

Arms Race and Disarmament

Specific issues of armament and disarmament are discussed in National Academy of Sciences (U.S.), *Nuclear Arms Control: Background and Issues* (1985); Curt Gasteyger, *Searching for World Security: Understanding Global Armament and Disarmament* (1985); and William T. Lee and Richard F. Staar, *Soviet Military Policy*

Since World War II (1986). Divergent views on the future of nuclear weapons are found in Keith B. Payne, *Strategic Defense: "Star Wars" in Perspective* (1986); Craig Snyder (ed.), *The Strategic Defense Debate: Can "Star Wars" Make Us Safe?* (1986); James H. Wyllie, *European Security in the Nuclear Age* (1986); Donald M. Snow, *The Necessary Peace: Nuclear Weapons and Superpower Relations* (1987); Angelo Codevilla, *While Others Build: A Commonsense Approach to the Strategic Defense Initiative* (1988); and especially Freeman Dyson, *Weapons and Hope* (1984). Robert M. Lawrence, *Strategic Defense Initiative* (1987), is a bibliography.

The End of the Cold War

The Reagan administration's foreign policies are documented in the memoirs of Ronald Reagan, *An American Life* (1990); Caspar W. Weinberger, *Fighting for Peace: Seven Critical Years in the Pentagon* (1990); and Peter Schweizer, *Victory* (1994). David E. Kyvig (ed.), *Reagan and the World* (1990), contains contrasting scholarly judgments. Michael Pugh and Phil Williams (eds.), *Superpower Politics: Change in the United States and the Soviet Union* (1990), explores the transition in policy from Reagan to Bush. The Bush administration is analyzed in Michael R. Beschloss and Strobe Talbott, *At the Highest Levels: The Inside Story of the End of the Cold War* (1993).

The "new thinking" in the Soviet Union was treated by numerous authors in the late 1980s, but events always outran their observations. Interpretations of the period include Peter Juviler and Hiroshi Kimura (eds.), *Gorbachev's Reforms: U.S. and Japanese Assessments* (1988); Tsuyoshi Hasegawa and Alex Pravda (eds.), *Perestroika: Soviet Domestic and Foreign Policies* (1990); Alfred J. Rieber and Alvin Z. Rubinstein (eds.), *Perestroika at the Crossroads* (1991); and Jiri Valenta and Frank Cibulka (eds.), *Gorbachev's New Thinking and Third World Conflicts* (1990). A thoughtful overview of these revolutionary years is William G. Hyland, *The Cold War Is Over* (1990).

Timothy Garton Ash, *The Magic Lantern: The Revolution of '89 Witnessed in Warsaw, Budapest, Berlin, and Prague* (1990), is an eyewitness narrative of the liberation of eastern Europe; while Charles Gati, *The Bloc that Failed: Soviet–East European Relations in Transition* (1990), offers a longer-range scholarly analysis. The integration movement and future of western Europe are treated in William Wallace, *The Transformation of Western Europe* (1990); Gary L. Geipel (ed.), *The Future of Germany* (1990); Françoise de La Serre, Jacques Leruez, and Helen Wallace (eds.), *French and British Foreign Policies in Transition: The Challenge of Adjustment* (1990); and Dennis L. Bark and David R. Gress, *Democracy and its Discontents, 1963–1991*, 2nd ed. (1993).

U.S.–Japanese tensions are the subject of Alan D. Romberg and Tadashi Yamamoto (eds.), *Same Bed, Different Dreams: America and Japan—Societies in Transition* (1990). The American role in Panama, Nicaragua, Chile, and other locations of the region is analyzed by Howard J. Wiarda, *The Democratic Revolution in Latin America: History, Politics, and U.S. Policy* (1990); and Dario Moreno, *U.S. Policy in Central America: The Endless Debate* (1990). Jamal R. Nassar and Roger Heacock (eds.), *Intifada: Palestine at the Crossroads* (1990), studies the Arab–Israeli conflict in the 1980s.

Contrasting views in the debate on the decline of the "American century" are presented in Paul Kennedy, *The Rise and Fall of the Great Powers: Economic Change and Military Conflicts from 1500 to 2000* (1987); Richard Cohen and Peter A. Wilson, *Superpowers in Economic Decline: U.S. Strategy for the Transcentury Era* (1990); Henry R. Nau, *The Myth of America's Decline: Leading the World Economy into the 1990s*

(1990); and Michael E. Porter, *The Competitive Advantage of Nations* (1990). Three elder statesmen discuss the prospects for a new world order: Richard Nixon, *Beyond Peace* (1994); Henry Kissinger, *Diplomacy* (1994); and William E. Odom, *America's Military Revolution: Strategy and Structure After the Cold War* (1993). Jonathan Clarke and James Clad, *After the Crusade: American Foreign Policy for the Post-Superpower Age* (1995), is also of interest.

Index

Photo Credits